Bob Toski's Complete Guide to Better Golf

Bob Toski's Complete Guide to Better Golf

BOB TOSKI
WITH DICK AULTMAN

Illustrated by Jim McQueen

ATHENEUM / SMI   NEW YORK   **1987**

Copyright © 1973, 1974, 1975 by Sports Marketing, Inc.

Copyright © 1977 by Atheneum Publishers, Inc. and Sports Marketing, Inc.

All rights reserved

Library of Congress catalog card number 75-39958

ISBN 0-689-70592-1

Manufactured in the United States of America by

Kingsport Press, Kingsport, Tennessee

Published simultaneously in Canada by Collier Macmillan Canada, Inc.

First Paperback Printing March 1980

Second Printing November 1980

Third Printing September 1981

Fourth Printing April 1982

Fifth Printing August 1982

Sixth Printing March 1983

Seventh Printing December 1983

Eighth Printing April 1984

Ninth Printing October 1985

Tenth Printing April 1987

Table of Contents

Bob Toski

Bob Toski is widely regarded as America's top teacher of golf, with good reason.

During the past 20 years, Toski has given over 80,000 golf lessons, many of them to leading players on the men's and ladies' PGA professional golf tours. Among the scores of celebrities he has taught or played with are Bing Crosby, Sidney Poitier, Ted Williams, Perry Como, Joe Namath, Phil Harris, Jackie Gleason, George Blanda, Ken Harrelson, and Eddie Arcaro.

One of nine children of Polish immigrants, Toski started his golf career at the age of five as a shop boy at Northhampton (Mass.) Country Club. He twice went broke on the pro tour before winning six tournaments in 12 months including George S. May's World Championship of Golf in 1954. This carried a $50,000 first prize plus a guarantee of 50 exhibitions at $1,000 each. Thereafter, Toski achieved many more tournament successes before retiring from the tour in the early 1960s to concentrate on teaching.

Today, in addition to his heavy international teaching and speaking commitments, Bob is a member of *Golf Digest* magazine's Professional Panel; a best-selling author with his highly esteemed *The Touch System for Better Golf,* and Dean of Instruction for the highly popular Golf Digest adult golf schools that he helped to found. Recently he launched his personally designed line of irons and woods.

Bob presently makes his home in Miami, Florida, but spends much time at the Palmetto Dunes Golf and Beach Club on Hilton Head Island, South Carolina, where he is Director of Golf.

The secret of Toski's success as a teacher lies in his ability to simplify the golf swing, and to impart its elements to the pupil in terms of physical "feel" rather than through semantical complexities and ambiguities. In this respect his power of communication is a major asset, as is his sympathy for and patience with the problems and aspirations of any golfer who truly wants to improve and is ready to work at it.

A born entertainer as well as an outstanding teacher, "The Mouse" — as Sam Snead calls Toski — exhibits unique credentials any time he takes a driver in his hand during a lesson or clinic. He can fly the ball at least 270 yards, which makes him, at 125 lbs., pound-for-pound unquestionably the longest driver in history.

Dear Fellow Golfer:

The instruction in this book represents a three-year effort on my part to produce a truly meaningful guide for the learning golfer. Much of the material herein first appeared in the instructional portions of limited edition Bob Toski Golf Diaries for the years 1974-1976. It is presented here under a single cover largely at the urgings of my friends who were unable to obtain any or all of these diaries.

This book is divided into three sections, in keeping with my belief that learning golf starts with applying certain vital fundamentals to one's address position and swing (Part One), then becomes an on-going effort to eliminate the specific causes of bad shots (Part Two), and, finally, culminates in developing the ability to visualize and duplicate successful swing patterns on the course during actual play. In Part Three, I analyze the swings of 12 outstanding players, all shown in high-speed movie sequences as model swing patterns to help guide you in this final visualization-duplication process.

I would like to thank Dick Aultman, fellow-teacher and former editor of *Golf Digest* , for his help in producing the original diaries and this book, and Jim McQueen for his outstanding artwork that appears herein. I sincerely hope that their efforts, and mine, will help you enjoy the game more than ever before.
Good golfing.

Bob Toski

PART 1: FUNDAMENTALS FOR BETTER GOLF

"No golfer is any better than his or her ability to apply certain fundamentals of address position and swing. That goes for Jack Nicklaus, Sam Sneed, Arnold Palmer, Johnny Miller and anyone else you might name. Learning the fundamentals requires clear understanding and hard work. Anyone who says otherwise is pulling your leg. However, once you've committed these basics to your 'muscle memory,' you'll be set for a lifetime of satisfying and enjoyable golf."

—Bob Toski

Right eye back, left hand forward

It's been said many times: "The way you set up to the ball directly influences the way you swing the club." I'll certainly endorse that statement, as would any golf instructor worth his PGA card. A good address position at least allows you to make a consistently good pass at the ball. A bad set-up . . . no way!

Thus it's not surprising that such super players as Tom Weiskopf, Jerry Heard, Lanny Wadkins and Johnny Miller — shown on the next three pages — all check their address positions almost every time they practice full shots. Their goal is to position themselves at address— before they swing—as closely as possible to the position they'll occupy, ideally, at impact. Why address the ball in one position and then shift into another during your swing? Needless movement reduces consistency. A consistent swing—even if it's not 100 per cent perfect— at least lets you plan your shots with a fair assurance that your ball will fly toward, and finish near, your chosen target.

Let's be specific. With only rare exception, you will strike the ball farther and straighter if: (1) your left hand leads your clubhead through impact, while (2) your head remains well behind the ball. "Left hand forward, right eye back"—that's the relationship I feel you should copy from these top professionals; that you should establish with the back of the ball BEFORE you begin your backswing. Reproducing

this relationship through impact will help you to deliver the clubhead to the ball while it is moving straight down the flight path at top speed.

Let's do it with mirrors. Set yourself up in front of a mirror—full-length, if possible—with some sort of vertical line behind you appearing in the glass. This vertical line may be the edge of a door, a groove in the wood of a panelled wall, or a stripe of tape running from floor to ceiling.

Position yourself so that the bottom of the line appears in the mirror just inside your left heel, where—ideally—you would play the ball within your stance. Set up so that your forward hand appears forward of this line. When thus positioned, this hand should block some of your left inner-thigh from view. Set your head so that at least your right eye is positioned behind the vertical line. Sense this positioning—memorize how it feels—until you can duplicate it at will.

Now I'm going to tell you how to look at the ball from your new address position. This is vitally important. The WAY you set your head at address is certainly as crucial as WHERE you set it. The way your eyes are positioned, for example, not only determines how you aim —or mis-aim—the clubface, but also the path on which you swing the clubhead.

Set yourself as I've described in front of the mirror. Now look down at the ball position and close your left eye. Next, turn your chin slowly

Great players such as Tom Weiskopf (shown here); Jerry Heard (page 16) and Lanny Wadkins and Johnny Miller, (top and bottom, page 17) all pull the clubhead through impact with their left hands leading and their heads remaining well behind the ball. Note how all of them preview this impact position in the way they set up at address.

to your right, so that it gradually points farther and farther behind the ball. Continue this turning until just before your nose begins to block your vision of the ball's position.

Once you've reached that point, turn your right cheek in slightly toward your right shoulder. Turn it just enough to allow yourself to look at the **back** of the ball, rather than the top of the ball. Finally, open your left eye. You should now feel that a line across your eyes would extend slightly to the right of your target.

What have we now accomplished? First, we've set your hands and your head in their proper impact relationship. Second, we've moved your chin into a position that will allow you to make a full and free backswing turn of your shoulders.

Third, we've set your eyes in a position that will encourage you to attack the ball with your clubhead moving along the correct path at impact, that being from inside to along the target line, rather than across that line from outside to inside.

Your new "touring pro" address position may feel strange at first. In no time at all, however, it will begin to feel comfortable and normal. And I think you'll like the way it enables you to connect with the ball.

Progress starts with proper posture

We are all creatures of habit. Consider, for instance, exactly how you are now sitting, or standing.

You are probably in a relaxed position, and you probably feel pretty comfortable. Now, shift yourself into a proper posture. Fit your bottom and your spine to the configuration of the chair or sofa you're in, or straighten up fully if you are standing. The new position may not feel uncomfortable, but I bet you it feels different. And I'll also bet you that, within a very short time, you'll fall back into the more natural sitting or standing position that you had found yourself in originally.

In this lesson I'd like to show you how to assume proper golfing posture, similar to that shown in the photos of pro tour stars Tom Weiskopf on the facing page and Johnny Miller and Lanny Wadkins on the next two. Your new posture may feel strange at first, which is why I've just asked you to experiment with your present body positioning. I want you to be aware of the normal human tendency to quickly fall back into old habits, to return to comfortable and familiar positions. I want you on guard against similar regression when you assume your address position on future golf shots.

How should you feel over the ball prior to swinging? I think I can impart proper posture to you if you will follow closely this simple drill:

1. Stand sideways in front of a mirror with your feet together, your back straight but relaxed, and your arms and hands extended in front of your chest with your palms open and touching together.

2. Look straight ahead, not up or down.

3. Slowly bend forward FROM YOUR HIPS so that your head, arms and hands gradually lower AS A RESULT of this bending. Keep your spinal cord straight as you bend—don't slouch your back or droop your head. As you bend you should feel your stomach move in and your bottom start to protrude to the rear.

4. Continue this bending until your eyes are looking at the spot where your golf ball would normally be positioned, then stop.

5. Spread your feet their normal width apart for making a full golf shot, then flex your knees slightly—just enough so that you can alternately raise and lower your heels.

6. Slide your right palm down your left into normal gripping position. As you do so, ease your right knee slightly inward toward your left knee — thereby slightly lowering your right hip and shoulder. But try to ensure that your hips and shoulders do not turn counter-clockwise as you make this move.

Excellent address posture is a big factor in allowing players such as Tom Weiskopf (facing page), Johnny Miller (next page) and Lanny Wadkins (page 21) to achieve great freedom of arm and leg movement during the swing. Note each player's slight knee-flex and relatively straight lower-back, with buttocks protruding and arms hanging almost vertically.

7. Turn your head toward the mirror to check your over-all posture. It should look similar to that of the golfers shown in the accompanying photographs.
8. Consciously examine how you feel in this address position. Primarily, you should feel a slight tension in your legs and lower back, but none in your shoulders and arms.

Practice this drill from start to finish until you can readily step into the final position without going through the step-by-step process. Then review the previous lesson on

hands and head positioning and apply it to your new set-up posture.

If all this stress on address position may seem a little tedious, let me say that, if you can improve your set-up, you will vastly improve your swing—**automatically and without question.** You can save yourself hours of practice time that you might otherwise spend on swing mechanics. Good posture, for instance, will reduce upper body tension and allow your arms to swing freely. As a result, you will coil your shoulders fully and freely without any conscious effort. Good posture will also put your swing on the correct plane—again automatically—for squarer striking of the ball more frequently. Good posture will allow you to swing without swaying or lifting your head.

In teaching and observing thousands of amateur golfers, I've found that about 95 per cent of them inhibit proper swinging of the club because of faulty address positions. If you will follow the advice I've given in this and the previous lesson, I guarantee that you will quickly join the elite five per cent who are ready to reduce their scores substantially and permanently.

Imagine, if you will, that you have a ping-pong ball sitting on this book in front of you. Your goal is to propel that ball across the room as far as you possibly can. I'll give you a choice of two methods. Take your pick.

Method 1: clench your fist, tighten your arm and bash the ball forward.
Method 2: coil your middle finger as tightly as possible against your thumb, then simply flick the ball forward.

The better technique is quite obvious — you'll propel the ball much farther with your finger than with your fist. Why? The answer is **speed.** You can flick your finger much faster than you can drive your fist. And similarly in golf, speed of movement, rather than brute force, best drives the ball forward. I weigh under 125 pounds. I can easily drive a golf ball 275 yards. Show me a 300-pound weightlifter who can muscle that little ball nearly.so far.

But let's forget about Toski and talk about you. Within your right hand and right arm you have a certain amount of strength — probably enough to roll a cannonball across

Sam Snead (shown here) builds club-head speed and avoids muscling the ball by keeping his right arm "soft" and hinged at the elbow well into his down-swing. Only after impact does the momentum of the clubhead force Snead's right arm to straighten. On the next two pages, we see Tom Weiskopf and Johnny Miller employing this same distance-adding technique.

your desk. You also have, in that hand and arm, the ability to create motion: to fling a 1.62-ounce golf ball out the window and far into the distance. Your problem, as I see it, is simply how to best apply your ability to create that fast motion to your golf swing. One way is to adopt the technique used by such great players as Sam Snead (shown here) and Tom Weiskopf and Johnny Miller (following pages).

One reason these outstanding golfers hit the ball so far is simply because subconsciously they do not associate distance with muscle power. Muscle power requires tension, but tension inhibits motion. So let's first build motion—speed of movement—by reducing tension, especially in your right hand, wrist, arm and shoulder. These are the areas where tension is most likely to stifle your ability to produce maximum clubhead speed.

Try the following drill the next time you are on the practice tee or at the driving range. It's designed to give you a feel for just how much tension you should have in your right hand, wrist and arm when you swing a golf club.

Take a 5- or 6-iron from your bag. Hold it lightly in just your right hand and start hitting balls that you have teed. At first you may miss the ball completely, but don't worry about that. After a few swings you'll start making contact. On each shot, sense how the club feels in your hand when it strikes the ball, and check how the ball flies. You may find that the ball feels heavy when you strike it, and it will probably fly or run to the right of where you've aimed. You may also top a lot of shots, causing the ball to nosedive.

These are all indications that either before or during your swing you are "over-controlling" the club with your right hand, arm or shoulder. The clubface will consistently return squarely to the ball only after you learn to "de-control" your influence on the club-shaft. To begin to "feel" how to do that, hold the club with even less grip pressure, and maintain that same light hold—no grabbing—throughout your swing. Let the club swing itself freely THROUGH the ball, without your

shoving or pushing it downward and forward AT the ball.

Once you sufficiently de-control your influence on the club, you'll finally start making square contact. The ball will feel light. It will fly straight, and much farther than you'd ever thought possible with a one-handed swing. Then, and only then, should you add your left hand to the club.

Now, as you swing with both arms, continue to strive for the same sensations of lightness and softness in your right hand, arm and shoulder area that you cultivated with the one-handed practice. Let your left hand and arm control the club while your right side remains soft and gentle.

In time, with practice, as you learn to SWING the club—not pressure it—you will automatically add motion and speed of movement to your swing. Gradually your shots will begin to fly farther and straighter than ever before—more like those of Messrs. Snead, Weiskopf and Miller.

Set angle...

Think for a moment about all the things you do with your right hand and arm during the course of a normal day. You shave, brush your teeth, cut food, write your name, open doors, lift the telephone, turn on the television, adjust the radio dial, and so on. The list is endless.

If you were to multiply all the things you do with your right hand by the number of times you do them, I think you would appreciate just how right-side oriented you really are. I'm sure that most right-handed people have more strength in their right hand than their left. I'm even more certain that they have developed superior right hand dexterity and sensitivity.

No wonder, then, that the right hand, right arm and right shoulder area dominate the golf swings of most players. No

..Retain angle

wonder most people rely so heavily on the side of their bodies which serves them best in so many ways. Not only does this side provide their main source of strength, but also their best means of control. And that's significant, because subconsciously most of us feel we must **control** the club to return it squarely to the ball, even though it's moving at close to 100 miles per hour. Subconsciously, most of us seek this control—plus the power we feel we need to drive the ball far—from our right hand, arm and side.

Golf, however, is a bilateral game. When one side dominates the other to any great degree, the player is certain to lose distance or accuracy, or both. Thus, no golfer can ever play his absolute best until he learns to either subordinate his right

Johnny Miller (shown here) and Jerry Heard (next page) exemplify setting "The Angle"—cocking the wrists—during the backswing, and retaining the resulting hinge in the shoulder-to-clubhead lever well into the downswing. They control setting and retaining this angle largely with the last three fingers of the left hand. Their right-hand grips are relatively light and passive throughout the swing. Most average players would benefit from emulating Miller and Heard.

side, or build up his left to the point where it will work more or less on equal terms with the right side.

This leads me to "The Angle," a concept developed largely by my friend and fellow-teacher, Jim Flick. The Angle is shown in the accompanying photos of Johnny Miller and Jerry Heard.

It's formed by the left arm and the clubshaft during the backswing and retained well into the downswing.

The Angle relates to left side control, in that good players like Miller and Heard set it largely with pressure in the last three fingers of the left hand. This pressure forces the right wrist and right elbow to fold, thereby helping to break down right-side dominance.

Retaining The Angle well into the downswing—again with the left hand in control—delays the maximum release of centrifugal force until near impact, so that the clubhead moves through the ball at maximum speed. When the right hand and arm take over and break down the left during the downswing, The Angle disappears too soon, centrifugal force is not maximized, and the clubhead decelerates into the ball. However, too much pressure on the clubshaft with either hand can retain The Angle too long. Centrifugal force is then not fully released until after impact— if at all. A weak, sliced shot is the usual result.

To help you to learn to set and retain The Angle and, in so doing, build up the role your left side plays in your golf swing, I recommend that you hit 7-iron shots, with the ball teed, using about a three-quarter swing. Don't worry about distance. Hold the club lightly in both hands, but mostly with the last three fingers of your left hand.

On your backswing, set The Angle—in other words, cock your wrists—very early with these last three left hand fingers. Then, during the downswing, try to smoothly accelerate your left arm through the impact area with your right hand and arm just going along for the ride. If you properly pace your downswing with your left arm, you'll have the feeling that your wrists are never going to release. They will, so long as you don't increase your grip pressure in the process. In other words, let the weight of the moving clubhead uncock your wrists.

Again, don't worry during practice about striking the ball very far. If your hands pass shoulder height on your follow-through, you're swinging too hard, with more right-hand and right-arm control than you need.

Swing is easy when legs feel 'kneesy'

Since we do so many things with our arms and shoulders during the course of daily living, it's only natural that most of us tend to rely heavily on our upper body and arm muscles to swing at a golf ball.

Unlike the pro tournament golfers shown on these pages, we are relatively unaccustomed to using our legs, except, of course, for the simple act of walking. Thus most amateur golfers don't think about their legs, don't know how to use their legs, and cannot easily sense the feeling of proper leg action. But the hard fact is that your legs are going to have to learn to play a starring role in your swing if you desire to become a really fine golfer, for with-

out them you are always going to lack power and balance.

Good footwork and legwork, like everything else in the golf swing, starts with the set-up, or address position. If you set up with too much weight on your heels or your toes, there is no way you can work your legs with maximum efficiency during your swing. I thus recommend that henceforth you set up with your knees flexed just enough so that most of your weight is on the balls of your feet—allowing you to alternately lift your heels in piston fashion while you address the ball.

A slight flexing in the knees at address will create a slight tension in your legs; just enough to tell you that they are willing and ready to move during the swing. Ideally, your legs should give you the feeling of being ready to coil and spring. All athletes who rely on quick response and fluid action or reaction seek a similar feeling of springy readiness in their legs—consider the outfielder in baseball, the linebacker in football, the tennis player awaiting his opponent's serve, the basketball player defending his basket. All flex slightly at the knees; none set back on their heels or forward on their toes.

For your legs to work properly during the swing, it is vital that you retain more or less the same amount of knee flex—in both legs—that you started with at address. If either leg straightens at any time prior to impact, you will lose mobility and balance and, in the end, distance and accuracy.

Should your right leg stiffen—should the right knee socket—during your backswing, there is no way you can drive your legs toward the target during the downswing. Without a downswing-initiating leg-drive, you must rely on your arms and shoulders to swing the club forward. Thereby you eliminate a major source of power, not to mention the lower body leadership that is so vital for swinging the clubhead on the correct path from inside to along the target line at impact.

Good players, like those shown here, work their weight toward the **inside** of their rearward foot during the backswing, and "spring" off of that foot during the downswing. Maintaining right-knee flex allows them to do this. When the rear leg straightens, during the backswing, your hips and shoulders will spin like a top; your weight will shift so far outside your right foot that you cannot recover and move it back to the left during your downswing; and you'll be forced either to "fire and fall back" onto your right side or lunge forward with your shoulders.

I think that the surest way to stifle proper legwork is to over-exert the shoulders. Show me a man who tries consciously to make a full shoulder turn on his backswing and I'll show you a man whose right leg stiffens. Show me a man who starts his downswing with his shoulders forcing the action and I'll show you a stiff left leg at impact.

I thus suggest that henceforth you avoid any conscious effort to turn your shoulders, but rather just allow them to follow the swinging action of your arms. Let your arms swing freely and keep a little knee-flex throughout your action. You'll be surprised how much more fluid and controlled your swing motion becomes — and how much farther your shots fly.

Study the swings of Lanny Wadkins (page 29), Johnny Miller (opposite page) and Tom Weiskopf (below) and you'll note a characteristic common to almost all top golfers: the right leg remains flexed from address throughout the backswing and well into the downswing. Such flexing adds distance by facilitating correct lower-body action, and is essential to initiating the downswing with the legs instead of the shoulders.

Sam Snead turns his shoulders fully, both going back and swinging through. So do Tom Weiskopf (page 34) and Johnny Miller (page 35). But the important point to note is that these great golfers turn fully as a RESULT of simply swinging their arms freely back and through. Consciously laboring the shoulders into a full turn can cause too much tension and thus inhibit correct arm and leg action.

All good golfers make a full-shoulder-turn on their back-swing. Right? **Right.** All good golfers CONSCIOUSLY make a full shoulder turn. Right? **Wrong!**

While some top players may, on occasion, work on coiling their shoulders fully, most couldn't care less if they turn 80 degrees, 90 degrees or 120 degrees.

It is true that in the photos accompanying this article we see the players' backs to the target at the top of their swings and their stomachs to the target at the finish. I contend, however, that in a proper golf swing the shoulders should always be followers, never leaders.

Nasty things happen when a golfer leads his swing with his shoulders. I've described how over-exerting the shoulders forces the legs to stiffen, which stifles proper

Back to TARGET, stomach to TARGET

legwork. Laboring the shoulders also make it difficult to maintain balance, by preventing you from working from the insides of your feet. Excessive shoulder turning thwarts smooth swinging—you have much less sensitivity for smooth motion in your shoulders than you do in your arms. Laboring with the shoulders also saps sensitivity from your hands, where you need a light touch to release the clubhead squarely into the ball at just the right time.

Imagine what would happen if your clubhead weighed, say, 10 pounds. Imagine how fully that much weight, swinging up and around your body, would coil your shoulders. Fortunately the clubhead doesn't weigh nearly that much. It does weigh enough, however, to force your shoulders to turn sufficiently in response to a free arm swing, if they are free of tension throughout your back-swing. And that, I am sure, is what happens to the shoulders of all the top golfers whom we see in this book.

Try this experiment, if you will. Stand facing a mirror with your arms hanging freely at your sides. Now, freely swing your arms back and forth in front of your body. Avoid tensing your shoulders as you swing. Let your body turn and your knees slide back and forth AS A RESULT of your arms swinging. Gradually lengthen the arc—back

and up, forward and up—on which you're moving your hands.

As you increase your arc, note how fully your shoulders turn as a result of your arms swinging. They'll turn even more when you swing a club—**so long as you don't inhibit their turning by allowing tension to creep in.** As you swing your arms in front of the mirror, suddenly clench your fists and tighten your arm muscles. I think you'll see immediately just how dramatically tension can thwart free and full turning of the torso.

The next time you play golf with friends, watch how much more freely and fully their shoulders turn —back to target, stomach to target —during their practice swings than during their actual passes at the ball. The difference is created by tension brought about by the presence of the ball. The subconscious urge to return the clubhead squarely to that little 1.68-inch object stifles freedom of motion and, as a result, full, free turning of the torso.

To develop the knack of swinging freely on actual shots, it helps greatly to think "target." Look at the ball, but concentrate most in your mind's eye on where you want it to go. Then simply swing the club THROUGH the ball and toward the target. You'll automatically make a freer arm swing, and your shoulders will turn fully as a result.

Point your way to straighter shots

Aided by photos of some great golfers, I'd like to show and tell you a bit about golf ballistics. Hopefully what I say might help you better understand why your shots often fly to the right or left instead of towards the target.

First, I'd like you to imagine a taut string extending from the target back to your ball and beyond. This is your "target line." Occasionally in my teaching I will actually lay down such a string to give my pupils a true visualization of this critical line. One thing this helps them to do is to aim the clubface squarely at the target before they swing. You may find it hard to believe, but it's true that many, if not most, golfers find it difficult to even aim the clubface properly.

Now, let's talk about the "initial flight path" of your shots. I refer to, say, the first 50 yards the ball travels. The initial flight path of any given shot is determined almost solely by the direction in which the clubhead is moving during impact. This is your first maxim of golf ballistics. If your ball starts out to the right of your target line, regardless of where it finishes, your clubhead was moving out to the right of that line—from inside to outside the target line—at impact. If your initial flight path is to the left of your target line, your clubhead was moving to the left—across the line from outside to inside—at contact. Of course, the ball may have curved right or left of that path once its high initial velocity began to decrease, but that was not caused by the path of the clubhead alone, as was the ball's **starting** direction.

Now, here's your second ballistics axiom: the direction in which a ball curves away from its initial flight path is determined by the direction the clubface is looking during impact. No matter in which direction the clubhead may be moving, if the clubface is looking to the **right** of that path, the ball will eventually leave the initial flight path and bend to the **right.** If the clubface looks to the **left** of the clubhead's path of movement, the ball will eventually curve to the **left** of its starting path.

In short, the path of the clubhead during impact determines the ball's initial flight path, and the direction in which the clubhead is looking during impact determines the direction in which the ball will bend off that path later in its flight. Naturally, the degree of bend is determined by the amount the clubhead is angled away from its path of movement (the greater the variation, the more curve-producing sidespin is imparted to the ball). If the clubface looks in the same direction the clubhead is moving, the ball will, of course, fly straight — although only on target if the clubhead was moving directly along the target line at impact.

Now, please study the accompanying photos. You will note that in each instance the initial flight path of the shot is more or less parallel to the direction in which the player's clubshaft was pointing at the top of his backswing. I find that among my pupils there is a definite correlation between where the clubshaft points at the the top of the backswing and the path on which the clubhead moves during impact. Thus clubshaft positioning at the top of the swing can be said to have a powerful influence on the ball's initial flight path.

If the clubshaft parallels the target line at the top, chances for swinging the clubhead along

The majority of top golfers attain accuracy largely be-cause, at the top of the backswing, they set the clubshaft more or less parallel to their intended line of flight. This relationship is shown in the photos of Lanny Wadkins on this page and Johnny Miller and Tom Weiskopf on fol-lowing pages. In each set of photos the actual initial flight path of the ball, shown in the right-hand picture, is superimposed on the left-hand photo of the player at the top of his swing.

that line during impact are vastly improved. If the clubshaft points to the left, the player will generally swing the clubhead from outside to inside the target line through impact, causing the ball to start out to the left. If the clubshaft points to the right, the player will generally start his shot to the right by swinging through the ball from in to out across the target line.

Thus, if your shots consistently start off line, ask a friend to check the direction in which your clubshaft points at the top of your swing. Should it not point parallel to your target line, first check the alignment of your shoulders at address, remembering that they should more or less parallel the target line. Next, consider the speed

of your backswing. Over-fast swingers tend to become too wristy at the top of the swing, frequently causing mis-aiming of the clubshaft. Finally, if your clubshaft still isn't properly aimed at the top, try cocking your wrists earlier in your backswing. Too delayed a wrist-cock can also tend to mis-aim the clubshaft at the top of the swing.

Remember that the prime reason for making a backswing is simply to place the club in position to make a proper forward swing. So consider taking it easy and setting the club in position gently, even if that means practicing with the shorter iron clubs until you can do so repeatedly. I promise you, the directional benefits will be immense.

Many times I've asked pupils to simply take a golf ball in hand and throw it forward, down the practice range. Almost without fail they will stride forward with their left leg as they swing their right arm back. And, of course, they will then firmly plant the left foot BEFORE they swing the throwing arm forward.

At least 90 per cent of my pupils will admit that they made the forward stride unconsciously. That's because it's an extremely natural move, made by any athlete throwing any object one-handed—a football, a baseball, even a javelin. It's also a natural move in many sports where the player is swinging an implement. The baseball batter, for example, strides into the pitch; the tennis player "steps into" his forehand stroke. Why does this happen? Very simply because, in both throwing and batting, the forward stride builds leverage that adds power to the motion being performed.

Golf is a different matter. For one thing, the ball is smaller and flies farther, which demands that it be struck very accurately. The striking implement itself is longer and thus more difficult to control than, say, a baseball bat or a tennis racquet. The hitting surface of the golf clubface is vastly smaller, of course, than the face of a tennis racquet. And, of course, the target area in golf—even on tee shots—is smaller than the target area in most other sports, especially on a length-to-width ratio. No wonder, therefore, that golfers don't stride into their shots. The chances for mis-hitting the ball are too great to permit this movement, however desirable it might be in terms of generating power.

Unfortunately, however, the need for a controlled striking action in golf too often leads to over-control. So conscious are we of our tiny targets that we guide or steer the clubhead back to the ball with our hands and arms, and in so doing we neglect the vast leverage-building potential we have in our legs. Ironically, by failing to use our legs, we also lose much of the accuracy we are seeking by steering the club with our hands and arms. Proper leg action early in the downswing, as shown in the accompanying photos, not only generates greater leverage—and thus more distance—but it also promotes accurate striking, by putting and maintaining the clubhead on a proper path to move squarely into the back of the ball.

What constitutes proper downswing leg action? In a nutshell, it consists of nothing more than a lateral sliding of the knees toward the target. The more this lateral or targetwards downswing knee-shift precedes the unwinding of the shoulders, the

Lead with your legs...

Three of golf's greatest "leg men"—Jerry Heard (below), Tom Weiskopf and Lanny Wadkins (top and bottom of next page) — all start their downswings by first sliding their knees laterally toward the target. Note in each set of photos that, while the player's legs have driven forward dramatically, his arms and clubshaft have moved little if at all.

more leverage the golfer builds, and the better his chance of returning the clubhead squarely to the ball from inside to along the target line.

Proper legwork on the downswing requires lightness afoot—as mentioned earlier, a feeling of springiness. Heavy-set golfers and players who do sedentary work, especially, lack this lightness—have "lazy legs." Jumping rope is an excellent remedy for the problem.

Proper knee action starts with proper footwork, and here's a drill to help you develop it. Simply swing your arms back and forth in front of you, and as you swing them back and up, shift your weight from the inside of your left toe to the inside of your right heel. Just before you swing your arms down and forward, shift your weight from your right heel back to the outside of your left toe. Keep swinging—toe-to-heel, heel-to-toe.

Be sure to keep both knees slightly flexed throughout this drill, and, once it feels natural, repeat it outdoors with a short-iron. Then take it to the practice tee and hit shots with the balls teed. Gradually lower the tee until you can make the same swing—with your flexed legs leading your downswing—when the ball is on the turf. The improvement in the quality of your shot-making, once you've mastered this maneuver, will amaze you.

...Follow with your shoulders

In the previous lesson I stressed the importance of leading the downswing with the legs, both to build distance-generating leverage and to put the clubhead on a proper path for maximum accuracy.

If your legs should be the first part of you to move during the downswing, the last should be your shoulders. The sooner your shoulders un-coil, the shorter you will drive the ball and the more likely you will be to mis-hit it. Check your own experience. Do your shots frequently start to the left of where you originally aimed the clubface? If the answer's yes, your shoulders are to blame. They are leading, not following, during your downswing.

Uncoiling the shoulders too soon in the down-

Jerry Heard, Johnny Miller and Lanny Wadkins not only avoid uncoiling their shoulders prematurely. Note in the ready back to their original address position (left-hand photos) while the shoulders have remained considerably coiled.

lead with their knees on the downswing, but also right-hand pictures how each player's knees are already back to their original address position (left-hand photos) while the shoulders have remained considerably coiled.

swing is one of the most common faults in golf. It happens so frequently because we are so accustomed to relying on our shoulders as a source of power in our everyday lives, whether we are mowing grass, shoveling snow, raking leaves, or polishing the car. It's only natural to call on the shoulders to power a golf ball, especially when distance is stressed. Restraining the shoulders requires, first, a retraining of the mind and body to perform unnaturally—until the unnatural becomes natural. The pros shown in the photos here have, obviously, mastered the technique.

For me to help you to retrain your shoulders, I must first motivate you by convincing you that doing so will give you longer golf shots. Therefore I'd like you to try this simple experiment, involving tossing a golf ball with about the same side-arm-underhand motion you use in your golf swing. First, throw the ball while keeping your legs as immobile as possible. Just plant your feet firmly on the ground and throw with only your shoulders and arms. Note how far the ball flies.

Now, throw another ball, but this time stride forward as you swing your arm back. Do not let your shoulders and arm swing forward until your lead foot is firmly planted. See if this throw doesn't go farther than the first. Also note the directions in which the two balls flew. If you are right-handed, I suspect the second toss flew to the right of the first. Why? Because by leading with your legs and thus restraining your shoulders, you automatically worked your right shoulder less out and around and more "under" yourself. In other words, you automatically swung your shoulders on a better plane for striking golf shots squarely.

I hope by now I've convinced you of the need to retrain your shoulders to act as followers. If so, I'd like you to continue throwing golf balls as you did on your second toss. Keep striding forward and restraining the forward thrusting of your shoulders. Then try hitting golf shots with a short-iron, at first with the balls teed. Continue striving to make your shoulders follow your legs and hips in the downswing.

I think you'll find that the farther you try to hit shots, the sooner you will uncoil your shoulders. Therefore, until you're well along in the retraining process, I suggest you try to hit your shots about 20 percent shorter than normal. And in doing that you just might find the ball flies as far, or farther, with only four-fifths of your normal effort.

While practicing as I've suggested, try also not to swing the clubhead too quickly off the target line during the takeaway. Moving the clubhead inside too soon, around your body, in the backswing may cause you to react by throwing it to the outside—away from your body —with your shoulders on the downswing. Envision the ball as being a clockface. Start the club back from it at "3 o'clock" and return it at "4 o'clock."

And here's a final tip to help you retrain your shoulders. Stand upright with your right arm hanging at your side, then gradually turn the arm clockwise. Note how your upper arm and elbow readily move in close to your side. If you can apply this same turning motion to the arm at the start of your downswing, I think you'll find it much easier to lead with your legs and follow with your shoulders. You may feel as though your clubhead is never going to catch up with your hands in time. Don't worry—it will.

Shots feel righ

46

I think it's unfortunate, but there is no doubt that some golf instruction terminology tends to mislead and confuse rather than enlighten and instruct improvement-conscious players. A prime example, to me, is the way we describe grip positions as being either "weak" or "strong."

Imagine that you are holding a club in your left hand, with your thumb on top of the club-shaft so that the back of your left hand, wrist and forearm from a straight-line relationship to the shaft. Many teachers, and most players, would call this a "weak" grip.

But look at the pictures that accompany this lesson. Note how the left hand-wrist-forearm relationship of these fine players closely approximates the straight line relationship we've just described, in both the pre-impact and impact photos. To me this is the ideal way to hold the club to produce both long and straight shots. And there is nothing "weak" about this position in my view.

Now, imagine that you are again holding a clubshaft in your left hand, but this time turn your hand so that you can see three or four knuckles. This is commonly called a "strong" grip. Note, however, the inward bending that this grip produces at the back of your wrist. This same cupping at the back of the wrist,

should it occur in your swing just before or during impact, will result in a weak shot. Your clubhead will decelerate before it reaches the ball. And your clubface will probably be mis-aimed during impact.

Thus here we have the problem of a so-called "strong" grip actually producing a weak impact position—while the grip that produces a strong impact position is labelled as being "weak." In my view, the sooner this piece of terminology is reversed, the easier it will be to teach people how to play better golf.

The purpose of this lesson is not to make you change your grip, but rather to stress the ideal impact position, which occurs when the back of your left hand, wrist and forearm is in more or less a straight-line relationship. Such a relationship is ideal because it indicates that your left hand, wrist and arm are still in control of the clubshaft. Don't here misunderstand the emphasis I'm placing on the left side. The right hand and arm do play an important part in the golf swing, but, as we've noted earlier, too much right side domination will not only expend clubhead speed too soon, but also throw the clubface off-line.

Many things can cause your right hand to take over and break down your left wrist prior to impact. Grabbing the clubshaft with the

Like most fine golfers, Johnny Miller (at left) and Sam Snead and Jerry Heard (following pages) pull the club down and through the ball with the back of their left wrist firm, straight and in control. Pressuring the club with the right hand—as most weekend golfers tend to do, usually in an effort to add distance— breaks down this firm left wrist, dissipates clubhead speed prior to impact, and mis-aligns the clubface.

when you lead with your left

right hand early in the downswing is an extremely common fault, the cure for which lies in consciously practicing maintaining a constant grip pressure. Rushing the downswing is another common problem. Try to start down slowly—leisurely even—with your left hand predominant in controlling the clubshaft. Trying for extra distance is another common cause of a player starting down too fast, with too much right-hand and right-side influence.

Similarly, too much concern about contacting the ball with the clubface often also leads to a premature forcing action with the right hand, in that it causes the player to try to flip the ball forward with the clubhead, throwing his right hand into the shot too soon and forcing a breakdown of the left wrist.

To build and maintain proper left-hand control, I suggest you practice shots with a short-iron club, say a 7-iron. Try to pace your for-

ward swing with your left arm. Never let your right arm outrace your left, or your right hand break down your left wrist. After impact, try to stop your swing before your hands reach shoulder height. Try to cut off your follow-through with your left hand and arm. This drill will gradually give you the firm left hand and arm you need through impact, and your reward will be crisper shots that fly both farther and straighter.

I think that one of the biggest hurdles any golfer faces in learning to play better is the inhibition that often occurs whenever he changes his normal pattern of gripping, setting up, or swinging.

Let's say you are working to improve your leg action—you're trying to swing with your knees flexed. Let's suppose your mind is currently focusing on maintaining a flexed right knee at the top of the backswing, that being the point where stiffening is most likely to occur.

Such a thought, though vital for the moment, can easily destroy the natural rhythm and motion of your over-all swing, with the result that you lose distance. Golfers who are looking for immediate success might well give up their efforts to improve leg action at this point, unable to resist the temptation to return to old, incorrect, but comfortable habits.

The wise student realizes that learning can be inhibiting, at least temporarily. He perserveres with the new technique, even though the immediate results are disappointing. He knows that, once the new positions and actions start to feel less foreign, his inhibitions will disappear and that his natural rhythm and motion will return.

There is a way, however, to short-cut this learning process and thus avoid much of the discouragement that comes when you inhibit your normal motion and rhythm. This is achieved by relating what you are trying to do DURING your swing to the POSITION it will produce on the "target side" of your swing. By simply swinging TO that specific target-side position, you automatically produce the alteration you seek during your swing, with little or no loss of rhythm and motion.

Obviously, you need some knowledge about cause and effect in the golf swing to be able to relate the specific alteration you are seeking to the specific position it should produce during, or at the end of, your follow-through. In this lesson and the next I'll try to give you this knowledge of cause and effect, in the hope that it will help you more readily master the instruction I've given you earlier.

Let's look at the accompanying photos. Note the "bowing" effect of the body that these players achieve during their follow-through. I call this the "Reverse C" position, since it looks like the letter C turned backwards. Most good players reach this positioning during the follow-through, with their heads still well back of the ball and their hips and legs shifted forward. Many less-skilled golfers' bodies would be in a more-or-less vertical "I"-like position at this point, with little or no inward bowing of the back and legs.

Jack Nicklaus (facing page) exemplifies the modern golf swing as he flows into the "Reverse C" position during his follow-through, a position that results from leading the downswing with the legs while maintaining a steady **head position well behind the ball. Other players in the Reverse C position on pages 52 and 53 are, from left to right, Jerry Heard, Johnny Miller, Lanny Wadkins and Sam Snead.**

The
'Reverse C'
for a swing
that's free

If you happen to be working on any of the following fundamentals, I suggest you study these photos, envision the "Reverse C" in your mind's eye—sense how it feels—and then try to actually swing into it during your follow-through.

One aspect of your action that swinging to the "Reverse C" will definitely help you to improve is your leg action. It is extremely difficult to reach this position if your right knee stiffens at the top of your backswing.

Swinging to the "Reverse C" position can also improve the timing of your downswing, by helping you to lead with your legs and follow with your shoulders. If

you start down with your shoulders un-coiling first, your legs will stiffen and you'll swing into the "I" position. Thus, if you are working on trying to maintain a steady head during your swing, con-sciously swinging to the "Reverse C" po-sition is excellent practice.

Finally, swinging to the "Reverse C" is a good way to train yourself to make a proper weight-shift during your back-swing. You'll discover that it's much easier to produce a "Reverse C" if your weight shifts to the inside, rather than the out-side, of your right foot as you swing your arms back and up.

Learning to do
what doesn't come naturally

In the previous lesson I made the point that pupils working on specific swing fundamentals may lose some of their natural swing rhythm and motion, at least until a new position or new pattern of movement begins to feel less foreign. The bad shots that result from such form-changes frequently discourage the student from persevering with the correction.

I stressed that you can minimize this loss of rhythm and motion, and still make the correction, by swinging TO the position on the target-side of your swing that the correction, when properly executed, automatically produces.

In this lesson I'm going to ask you to study two aspects of the finish positions of the players shown in the accompanying photos, and tell you which fundamentals swinging to these positions will help you to build into your golf stroke.

Please study each player at both of the camera angles shown in the photos. The first thing I'd like you to note is the positioning of each player's hands and arms. In each instance you will perceive that: (1) the player's hands are higher than his head, and (2) both arms are well to the left side of his head. None of the players are looking down the fairway between their arms.

The second point to notice is the positioning of each player's right leg and foot. All right knees point down the fairway. All right feet are up on the toes.

I suggest you study these photos and then make some practice swings in front of a mirror without a club in your hands. Practice swinging to these positions until you can reach them via a natural swinging motion, without consciously forcing yourself into any specific position. Once you achieve this capability, continue swinging while sensing how it feels to make this stroke. Try to "muscle memorize" the feelings you are experiencing in your arms, body and legs. Next, take a club in hand and try to duplicate these sensations as you swing without the mirror.

The final step is to hit practice shots—tee the ball at first—with the swing you have been practicing. Don't worry about the results of the shots. Simply swing to the finish positions I've illustrated with the same free swing you have muscle memorized.

This process will help you master many of the fundamentals I've discussed in these lessons, without too much sacrifice of rhythm and motion. It will help you, for instance, to swing your arms freely and swiftly THROUGH the ball instead of guiding or steering the clubhead TO it, because there is no way to swing freely to the finish positions I've highlighted if you are overly concerned about striking the ball squarely.

The results of free-swinging arms and free-turning hips and legs are clearly evident in the photos of (in order) Lanny Wadkins, Johnny Miller, Sam Snead and Tom Weiskopf. Note that in all cases the player's hands have finished high and well around to his left side. Almost all weight has been transferred solidly onto the left foot — no "fire and fall back" here.

Swinging to these positions will also help you to shift your weight properly onto your left foot at the start of your downswing, and thus retain "The Angle" we discussed earlier. Further, the exercise will help you to lead the downswing with your legs because, if you shove or push with your right shoulder, you will not be able to finish with your hands high above your head; if you try to scoop the ball upward you will not finish with your arms well to the left of your head; and if you start your downswing with your shoulders, you'll find it all but impossible to finish high on your right toe.

Swinging to these positions will help to train you to maintain a steady head during your swing. It will even help you to set your clubshaft parallel to the target line at the top of your swing, and thus allow you to swing the clubhead along the target line through impact.

I must inject here a word of caution, however. It's one thing to swing freely to a proper finish position when you're standing in front of a mirror or in your back-yard, and an entirely different story when you have a ball in front of you on the practice tee. And it's even more difficult to make a free, uninhibited, rhythmical swing on the course itself, where the ball may be sitting down in the grass, your stance may not be level, and every swing counts one stroke. It takes a lot of effort and a cool head to successfully take your swing from the practice tee to the battlefield. I sincerely hope these lessons have inspired you to make that effort. And I wish you the very best, both on and off the course.

PART 2: GOLFING PROBLEMS — CAUSES AND CURES

"Golf is a game of continual correction. Even the best players expect to mis-hit several shots per round. The intelligent player, however, is the one who has learned what specific mis-application of the fundamentals will cause a certain ill-effect on his or her shots. Armed with this knowledge of cause and effect, it becomes much simpler and quicker to put one's game back to normal."

— Bob Toski

BOB TOSKI'S CAUSE-and-EFFECT CHECKLIST

POSSIBLE EFFECT

	Poor Target Projection	Tense at Address	Weight too Far Left At Address	Ball too Far Back In Stance	Ball too Far Forward In Stance	Ball too Far Away At Address	Ball too Close at Address	Mis-aiming Left	Mis-aiming Right	Alignment Too "Open" At Address	Alignment Too "Closed" At Address
Slicing (pg. 60)		*	*		*					*	
Pulling (pg. 64)	*	*	*	*	*	*	*		*	*	
Hooking (pg. 68)				*					*		*
Pushing (pg. 71)	*			*	*			*			*
Topping (pg. 74)		*	*	*	*	*	*				
Fat Shots (pg. 78)			*		*		*				*
Shanking (pg. 82)		*					*				
Loss of Length (pg. 85)	*	*	*		*		*				
Shots too High (pg. 88)	*		*		*						
Shots too Low (pg. 91)		*	*	*	*	*					
Inconsistent Shotmaking (pg. 94)	*	*									
Bad Putting (pg. 98)	*	*				*	*		*		

"Strong" Grip	"Weak" Grip	Backswing Too Fast	Too Little Time at Top Of Backswing	Right Leg Stiff At Top of Backswing	Too Much Lift, Too Little Backswing Turn	Overswinging On Backswing	Grabbing Club (Overcontrolling) On Downswing	Right Hand/Arm Shoving on Downswing	Right Hand Throwing on Downswing	Falling Back On Downswing	Swaying From and/or To Target	Blocking Out With Hands	Blocking Out With Hips on Downswing
	*	*	*				*			*		*	
	*		*	*			*	*	*				
*						*			*				
*							*				*	*	*
		*	*	*	*		*	*	*		*		
		*			*	*			*	*			*
		*	*	*			*	*			*	*	
		*	*	*	*		*	*	*		*		
*						*			*	*			
	*				*		*	*			*	*	*
*		*	*		*	*	*				*		
		*	*			*	*		*		*		

59

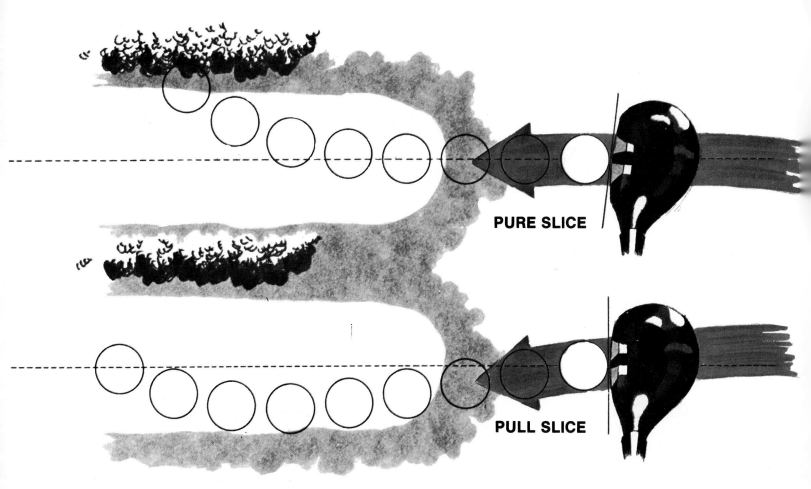

PURE SLICE

PULL SLICE

Causes and cures for
Slicing

To slice a shot, the clubface must be open to the clubhead's path of movement during impact. The "pure slice" starts flying straight on target because the clubhead is moving down the line. Then it curves right for righthanders. The "pull slice" starts left of target, because the clubhead is moving left, and then curves right. It usually flies lower than the pure slice.

Sliced shots are like weeds; they are all too common and, sometimes, difficult to recognize. Left untended they flourish to the point where they'll strangle your entire game.

The pure slice deceives no golfer. It starts on target and then spins way off toward trouble on the right. The player who hits this shot surely knows he's sliced.

The common garden variety slice, however — the pull-slice — often finishes in the middle of the fairway. The ball starts left, usually on a low trajectory, and then curves back towards the center of the fairway. Since it finishes in the short grass,

this type of slice often goes unrecognized for what it is — or, at least, uncorrected. The player resigns himself to living with it, even though he feels it to be an ugly and weak way to hit a golf ball.

Any shot that curves to the right is a slice, regardless of where it finishes, in that it is struck with the clubface open (looking to the right) of the clubhead's path of movement. If your slice starts straight and curves right, your clubface, though open, is at least moving *toward* the target when it contacts the ball. If your slice starts left, your clubhead at impact is moving to the *left of* target

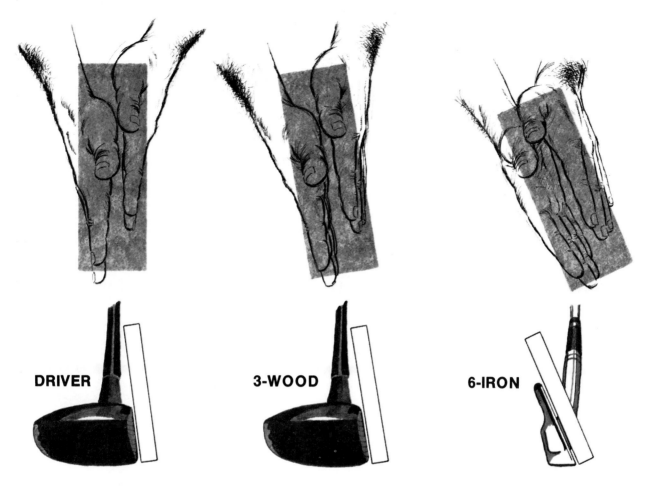

DRIVER **3-WOOD** **6-IRON**

Ideally, both palms should parallel each other on the clubshaft. The golfer whose palms align with a clubface of driver loft is more likely to slice than if his palms aligned at 3-wood loft. Chronic slicers may need to align their palms at approximately 6-iron loft on all shots in order to square the clubface by impact.

instead of straight forward. Then your problem is not only an open clubface, but also an improper clubhead path. The bend will manifest itself primarily on shots with the less-lofted clubs. The fact that you tend to pull your short irons to the left with little or no curve doesn't mean you don't have a slice swing with these clubs. You are a pull-slicer with every club, and you should thus study the instruction in the section on pulling as well as that which follows in this section.

Both the pure slice and the pull-slice cost you distance because in each case the clubhead faces to the right of its path of movement at im-pact, causing a glancing instead of a square blow. Of the two types, the pull-slice is the greatest distance-reducer because the clubhead, in making this kind of shot, moves steeply downward instead of directly forward — the force of the blow is toward the ground instead of the target. How-ever, although it may fly longer, the pure slice, be-cause it starts straight and curves right, is more likely to put you in the wilderness.

Obviously, the only way to cure slicing is to elim-inate the open clubface. Once your clubface align-ment and your clubhead path coincide, you will strike the ball squarely and it will fly without

Hand positioning may vary with the individual, even among top touring professionals. Johnny Miller (at left) sets his hands well to his left in a position that would cause most players to slice. Lanny Wadkins (center) positions his hands in a more orthodox position, while Lee Trevino (right) turns his well to his right.

curving. The pull-slicer, however, will continue to pull shots to the left until he also learns to swing the clubhead along the target line at impact.

There are several factors that might be causing your open clubface. However, because your hands directly affect your clubface alignment at impact, the first thing to check is the way you hold the club. As a general rule, the farther your hands are turned to your left on the club as you address the ball (to the right for southpaws), the more your clubface will tend to be open — face right — at impact. Thus your first step should be to hold the club with your hands turned farther to your right.

The ideal grip is one in which both palms would align with the clubface of your driver at address. As a slicer, however, you may need to align both hands more to the right of this ideal for the time being, so that your palms would align with the face-loft of your 5-iron or 6-iron. Do not, however, depart from the ideal to the point that the V's formed between your thumbs and forefingers point to the right of your right shoulder.

If you reposition your hands so that these V's point to your right shoulder, and, after one or two solid practice sessions, you are still slicing, you should maintain that grip and go on to the following additional corrections. All are designed to eliminate the open clubface, and I suggest you make them in the order they appear here, proceeding down the list until your slice disappears.

1. Hold the club lightly at address, especially with your right hand. Use no more grip pressure than is needed to merely suspend the clubhead slightly above the ground.

2. Try to maintain a constant, light grip pressure throughout your swing. Avoid, particularly, any "grabbing" during your downswing, because this is a sure way to prevent the clubface from squaring.

3. Slow the pace of your backswing and give yourself more time to make a leisurely change of direction from backswing into forward swing.

4. Do not let your wrists turn clockwise during the first three or four feet of clubhead movement away from the ball.

5. Try to hit your full shots about 20 per cent shorter than normal. You'll be surprised how far, and straight, they actually fly.

Causes and cures for
Pulling

At first glance, you'd think that one of the simplest things in golf would be to swing the clubhead toward the target. Even a child can toss a penny or a pebble fairly straight. I've seen great-grandmothers repeatedly roll a bowling ball down the middle of the alley. Yet, merely moving a golf clubhead down the target line through impact sooner or later becomes a major problem for every golfer. And, since pulled shots reflect this inability, it is no wonder that pulling the ball to some degree is such a common golfing disease.

In the case of the pure pull, the clubface is square to the path of clubhead movement during impact, but that movement is directed to the left of target. The ball doesn't curve sideways in flight, but its path of flight is always to the left. Also, because the clubface is square to the clubhead's

All pulled shots start left of target for righthanders because clubhead's path is in that direction. The "pure pull" curves little thereafter because clubface is looking in direction clubhead is moving. The "pull hook" curves farther left because clubface is closed to clubhead path. "Pull slice" starts left and curves right because clubface is open to clubhead path.

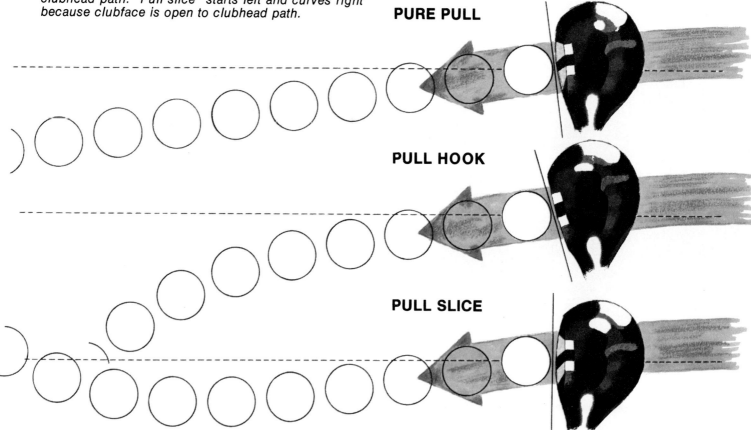

PURE PULL

PULL HOOK

PULL SLICE

path of movement when it meets the ball, the pulled shot feels solid. It flies far. Unfortunately, it flies in the wrong direction.

Closely related to this pure pull are the pull-slice and the pull-hook. In each case the ball also *starts* its flight to the left, in response to the direction in which the clubhead is moving during impact. Thereafter, however, the ball curves, either back to the right or farther to the left, depending on whether the clubface was opened or closed to its path of movement at impact.

If your pulled shots also slice or hook after starting to the left, to hit straight shots you must apply the corrections for slicing or hooking as well as those that follow. If your bad shots — especially those with the less-lofted clubs — simply fly left without much curving, the sugges-

Shoving right shoulder and arm outward causes duffer in drawing to swing clubhead across target line in typical pull-shot pattern. Jack Nicklaus works right shoulder under and keeps right elbow in, to swing clubhead from inside to along target line.

tions in this section should suffice.

You must understand from the start that for a shot to begin its flight toward the target, the clubhead *must* be moving directly along the target line during the milli-second in which it compresses and releases the ball. Actually, the clubhead can move *directly down* the target line for only a matter of a few inches. During the downswing it must approach the ball from the inside (your side) of the target line. Following impact, the clubhead will naturally return to the inside again as it swings around your body and upward on your follow-through.

The key point to remember is that, any time your clubhead moves *outside* (beyond) the target line *prior* to impact, it cannot be moving *down* the line at contact. Instead, it must be cutting back to the inside — to the left of target — when it meets the ball. Thus the stage is set for pulling, pull-slicing and pull-hooking at some point early in the downswing when you do something that throws or shoves the club away from your body toward the far side of your target line. The common phrase, "coming over the top," refers to this very common outward throwing or shoving among handicap golfers.

The obvious cure for coming over the top lies in somehow returning the clubhead back to the ball from *farther inside* the target line, so that the clubhead cannot be beyond it before impact.

I feel that a common cause of coming over the top is simply that of mis-aiming the clubface to the *right* of target at address. The golfer who aims to the right at the outset subconsciously realizes that somehow he must direct the clubhead back to the left during his forward swing, in order to bring it back on target. As a result, as he starts his downswing, he throws or shoves the club toward the outside to put it in position to swing back to the left. In short, aiming right and swinging left leads to coming over the top.

Proper aiming is thus the first step, and perhaps the only adjustment you'll need to cure pulling. One way to learn proper aiming is simply to lay two clubs on the ground *parallel* to your target line. Lay one club outside the target line, beyond the ball, and the other far enough inside so that

you won't strike it as you swing. Once you've built yourself this "channel" with the two clubs, merely square your clubface to them as you address the ball. If you have been aiming to the right, at first your clubface will look closed to the left even though it is demonstrably square. You must adjust to this visual impression by trusting the fact that your aim is now correct and by attempting to swing through the ball in that direction.

I find it also helps many golfers to aim properly if they use the vertical lines on the clubface, rather than its leading edge, as their alignment guide. It also is wise to occasionally ask a friend to stand behind your ball and check your aiming of the clubface.

Apart from aiming to the right, there are other causes of pulling, which are noted on the chart that accompanies these chapters (see pages 58-59). The corrections for the more common of these faults are as follows:

1. Play all full shots with the ball opposite a two-inch range off the inside of your left heel. Playing the ball too far back can lead to aiming right. Playing it too far forward can cause you to align your body too far left of target, and also encourage you to turn your hands too far to the left on the club as you address the ball. Your right hand then faces somewhat downward instead of forward, in a position all too likely to cause throwing the club outward at the start of your forward swing.

2 Set your weight more on the balls of your feet, rather than on your heels, at address. This will discourage falling forward onto your toes — a common cause of coming over the top.

3. Slow the pace of your backswing and try to extend its length. This will give you more time to change directions at the top — more time for your legs, rather than your shoulders, to lead your downswing. It will help to offset any tendency to shove your right shoulder forward during the downswing.

4. Try to strike your full shots 20 yards shorter than normal. Striving for extra length may be causing you to throw outward with your right hand, and/or shove your right shoulder over the top at the start of the downswing.

Laying two clubs on ground parallel to target line as shown here simplifies learning to aim clubface down the line during practice sessions. Proper aiming offsets common tendency of aiming right and then pulling shot to the left in a subconscious effort to bring it back on target.

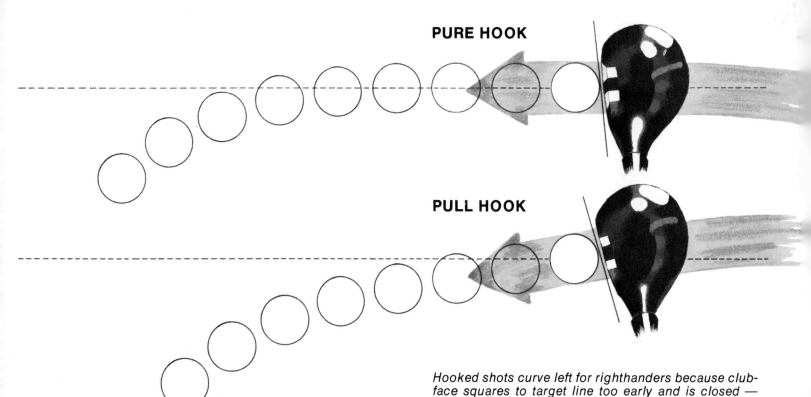

PURE HOOK

PULL HOOK

Hooked shots curve left for righthanders because clubface squares to target line too early and is closed — facing left — of clubhead path by impact. "Pure hook" starts on target because of on-line clubhead path and curves left thereafter because of closed face. "Pull hook" starts left because of outside-inside clubhead path and curves farther left because of closed clubface.

Causes and cures for

Hooking

One thing should be comforting to readers seeking help in this particular section: there is a good deal of truth to the common observation that just about all golfers with potential to excel do, at some time, go through periods of hooking.

This is true in part because anyone who can consistently curve the ball from right to left has the proven ability to readily square his clubface to the target during impact. When he swings naturally — lets it "all hang out" — he will not lose distance because of slicing, but rather will obtain the lower flight and extra roll that normally go with hooking.

The hooker's concern, therefore, is the comparatively simple matter of better controlling what he already does naturally. Specifically, he needs a way to avoid squaring the clubface *too soon,* prior to impact, so that it won't be closed (facing left of target) by the time it actually reaches the ball.

Only the pull-hooker, whose ball starts left and then curves farther left — the so-called "smothered hook" — needs additional help. If you tend to hit these "blue darters," your problem is not only hooking, but also pulling or "coming over the top." You will thus need to apply not only the corrections in this section, but also give attention

Hooking may result from insufficient hip turn on the forward swing. When the hips stop, the hands turn the clubface closed as shown in the drawing. Young Ben Crenshaw retains square clubface by clearing left hip prior to impact.

to those in the section on pulling.

There are two major reasons why hookers arrive at impact with a closed clubface. The first stems from failing to freely turn the left side out of the way during the downswing. When the left side slows down or quits turning, the left arm and hand also decelerate prior to impact, which allows the right hand to outrace the left and turn or throw the clubface into a closed position. The clubface then not only arrives at the ball facing somewhat left of target, but also — because it is turned "in" — somewhat de-lofted. Thus hooks not only curve left; they also fly lower than normal.

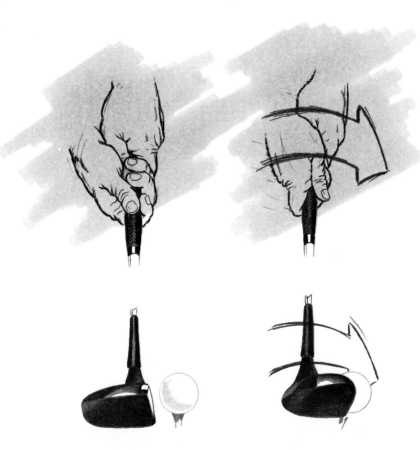

It is natural for the right palm to return to an on-target facing at impact (drawing on right). This will close the clubface and cause hooking if, at address (drawing on left), this hand is too far under the clubshaft.

In my book *The Touch System for Better Golf,* I describe the lower-body action in the swing as being a "turn-slide-twist." During the backswing the hips should *turn* to the right. At the very start of the downswing the hips and legs should *slide* laterally toward the target. This should be followed immediately by a *twist* to the left. While the pull-hooker needs more slide, to avoid coming over the top, the pure hooker needs more twist. He slides sufficiently, but thereafter his legs and lower body go dead allowing his left hand and arm to decelerate before impact, which in turn allows his right hand and arm to take over and close the clubface.

Thus, if you are a pure hooker, work on twisting your hips to the left sooner on your downswing. Accelerate your left arm freely forward through impact. Let your left side and left arm set the pace. Toeing out your left foot 30 to 45 degrees at address will help you to accelerate your twist.

The second major cause of hooking is holding the club at address with the hands turned too far to the right. The back of the left hand and the palm of the right face too much skyward instead of targetwards. This is known as a "strong" grip because it simplifies turning the clubface to the left — a squaring action — during the forward swing. Unfortunately for the hooker, who already excels in that maneuver, the strong grip over-encourages such turning. Thus the clubface becomes squared too soon and is applied to the ball in a closed alignment.

Moreover, a strong grip can lead to a "weak" impact position. The farther the left hand is turned to the right at address, the more likely the golfer will return to impact with the back of his wrist broken down and cupped inward, a position that can lead to slicing, skying and topping, as well as hooking.

Hookers, therefore, should hold the club at address with the back of their left hand and the palm of their right hand facing more toward the target — less skyward. This grip change will counteract the tendency to turn the clubface to the left too soon, and should also produce a firmer, straighter, more stable left wrist through impact.

If additional hip "twist," and, perhaps, the grip change, do not keep your shots from curving left, I suggest you also:

1. Play the ball a bit farther forward — toward the target — in your stance.

2. Maintain a light but *constant* pressure between the heel pad of your right hand and the thumb pad of your left, both at address and throughout the swing.

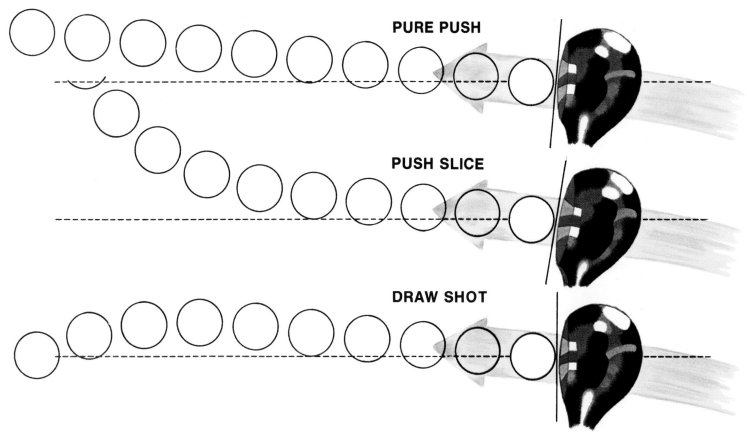

PURE PUSH

PUSH SLICE

DRAW SHOT

All pushed shots start out to the right of target because the clubhead is moving across the target line in that direction during impact. Thereafter the ball will fly in that same direction (pure push), curve farther right (push slice) or curve left (draw shot) depending on whether the clubface's alignment is identical to the clubhead path or open or closed to it.

Causes and cures for
Pushing

The push is one of those shots that feels good but looks bad. Though highly penal on tight courses, it does offer the consolation of having resulted from a number of correct moves. Perhaps for that reason it is one of the least common of the bad shots.

The pushed shot is one that, for righthanders, flies to the right of target with little or no bend in either direction. To push a shot to the right, you must start the club back to the ball from well inside the target line, which is the feature that indicates that you are doing something right. What makes the shot go wrong is the fact that, during impact, the clubhead is still moving from inside, rather than along, the line. Since the clubhead is moving to the right of the target, the ball starts out in that direction. And, since the clubface is square to the path of clubhead movement, the ball usually flies far with little curve. The ball is usually squarely struck, which is why the shot feels better than it looks.

Normally the golfer who manages to start the club down from well inside the target line "releases" his arms and wrists freely through impact, which squares the clubface to the *target* by impact. The result, of course, is the highly respectable "draw" shot, wherein the ball starts slightly right, curves gently back toward the target and, generally, provides excellent distance.

Unless his shots are starting out extremely far to the right, all that the pusher needs to learn is to freely square his clubface to the target by impact. Once he manages that, he'll draw his shots elegantly as I've just described.

I feel that there are two main reasons why pushers fail to freely square the clubface and, in some instances, actually swing from too far inside the target line.

The first cause is swaying the entire body toward the target on the forward swing. The player properly makes a full backswing turn to the right, which sets the club well inside the target line. Then, however, he fails to make a completely

Swaying the upper body toward the target on the forward swing promotes pushing. Clearing left hip while holding head back in position, as Tom Weiskopf has done here, helps clubhead swing along target line during impact.

72

reciprocal *turn* to the left coming down and through. Instead he *slides* everything — even his head — laterally in the direction of the target, which causes him to shove the ball way out to the right.

If swaying is your problem, you must make a conscious effort to turn your hips to the left early in your downswing. At the same time, try to ensure that your head stays in place, which is well back of the ball. This double effort may throw your timing off temporarily, especially if you tend to start your downswing turn before you finish your backswing, but stick with the correction in your practice sessions. If you find it difficult to turn to the left in your downswing, open your stance slightly and turn your left toe a little more to the left (toward the target) at address.

The second major cause of pushing is over-controlling the club — *shoving* it forward instead of freely *swinging* your hands and arms down and through. Free swinging will automatically square your clubface to the target by impact. Shoving leaves the clubface open to the right, causing a pure push or even a push-slice. The main culprit here is too much increase of grip pressure — "grabbing" — during your forward swing.

The best way to eliminate over-control of the club is by practicing a mini-swing. Tee the ball and play it opposite your left heel. Take a seven-iron and hold it lightly, especially with your right hand. Cock your chin slightly to the right before swinging. Then merely hit short shots — 20 to 30 yards — by simply cocking and uncocking your wrists.

If you maintain a light grip pressure as you make this short stroke, your clubface will square itself to the target every time and the ball will start to fly straight. If your shots continue going right, you need a still-lighter right-hand grip *throughout* your forward swing, along with more turning of the clubface to the left with your *left* forearm and hand.

Continue this drill until you are striking the ball crisply and squarely forward. Sense the rotation of your left forearm to the left — counterclockwise — during your forward stroke. Then gradually increase the length of your swing, but *not* your right-hand grip pressure. Tee the ball lower and lower until you are finally playing from the turf itself.

Eliminating the sway, and/or working on a mini-swing, should bring your pushed shots back on target. If not, try the following suggestions:

1. Make sure you play the ball opposite the inside of your left heel. Playing it too far forward encourages swaying. Playing it too far back may not allow your clubhead enough time before impact to return from inside to along the target line.

2. Ask someone to check your original aiming of the clubface. Aiming left causes a subconscious reaction to push right. Aiming right can, occasionally, mislead you into simply misdirecting your shots in that direction.

Swinging the arms forward freely, as Bruce Crampton does here, helps rotate clubhead into square-to-target facing during impact. A light grip pressure leads to this free-swinging. Grabbing clubshaft on downswing thwarts free forearm rotation and leaves clubface open at contact.

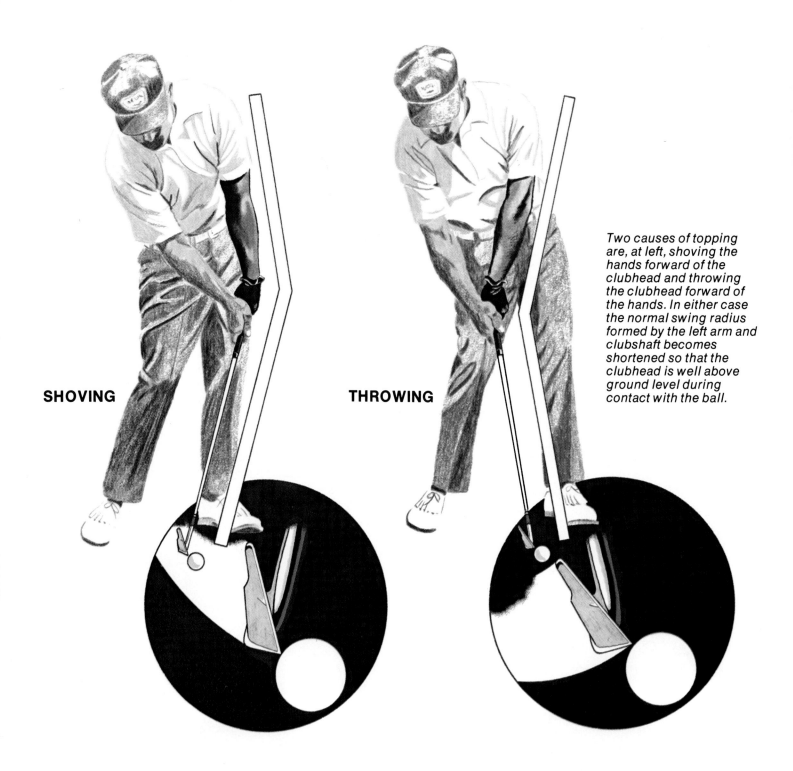

SHOVING

THROWING

Two causes of topping are, at left, shoving the hands forward of the clubhead and throwing the clubhead forward of the hands. In either case the normal swing radius formed by the left arm and clubshaft becomes shortened so that the clubhead is well above ground level during contact with the ball.

Jack Nicklaus achieves square contact by re-establishing at impact the swing radius, formed by his left arm and clubshaft, that he first established at address.

Causes and cures for

Topping

Most reasonably experienced golfers top or hit shots very "thin" once or twice a round at most. Topping seldom hangs in so persistently as slicing, pulling or — perish the thought — shanking. It should be treated, however, even in its mildest forms, because it does, in fact, indicate swing faults that can lead to much more severe trouble.

Also, topping is a particularly pesky problem because, like shanking, it happens most often on short shots around the green. Top a fairway wood

and you may still have a chance to recover on the hole, but skull a short pitch shot across the green and invariably you'll be scrambling for a par or worse from deep grass or trees, often it seems to a downhill putting surface.

The end-cause of topping is simply striking the ball too high on its perimeter. The shot, void of backspin, nosedives quickly or scoots along the top of the grass, worm-high.

There are two basic varieties of a topped shot,

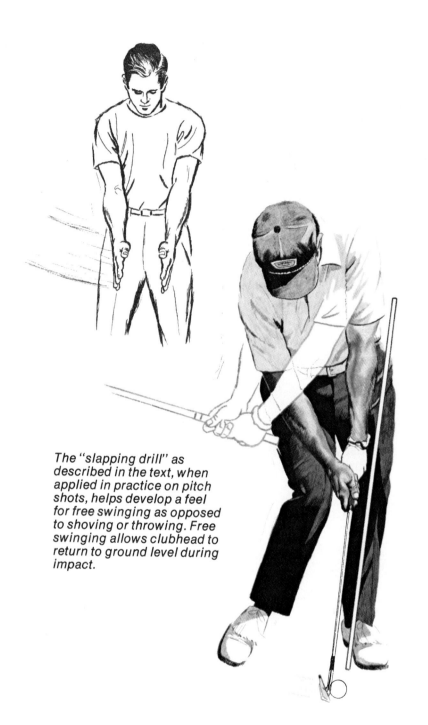

The "slapping drill" as described in the text, when applied in practice on pitch shots, helps develop a feel for free swinging as opposed to shoving or throwing. Free swinging allows clubhead to return to ground level during impact.

Gary Player re-establishes his left arm-clubshaft radius gradually during his downswing, largely because he swings his arms down and forward freely without shoving with his right shoulder or suddenly grabbing the shaft with his right hand.

and each has its own causes. One type occurs when the clubhead chops steeply down on the ball, contacting its topside before cutting into the turf. The other type occurs when the leading edge of the clubhead catches the backside of the ball while it is moving upward at the start of the follow-through. The low shot that I discuss in a later section is a less severe form of this type of topping.

Whether you top shots because of a steep downward chop or an upward lift of the clubhead, one thing is certain: in either case you have failed to re-establish by impact a correct swing radius as formed by your left arm and clubshaft. Something has caused you to either shorten this radius, or to lift it, prior to striking the ball.

The chart that precedes this instruction (see pages 58-59) lists the more common ways that golfers shorten or lift their swing radii. I feel, however, that the most prevalent cause is grabbing onto the clubshaft with the right hand prior to impact.

Grabbing the club thus can alter the swing radius by forcing the left arm to bend at the elbow or at the back of the wrist. In either case, the

clubhead moves upward too abruptly before impact. Grabbing with the right hand also creates right-arm and right-shoulder tension that stifles free swinging. Instead, the hands are *shoved* forward with the wrists still slightly cocked at impact. This again is a common cause of shortening the swing's radius, in that the clubhead never returns to ground level.

One way to overcome grabbing with the right hand — and thus achieve both the proper radius and a freer swinging motion — is by simply learning to slap freely with your right hand. Start by extending your left arm and hand — fingers together — in front of you, with the back of the hand towards the target. Now, slap its palm with your right hand and wrist. Notice that the greater the tension, the more your slap becomes a shove. Learn to slap with practically no tension.

Next, apply this same right-hand slapping motion, with club in hand, during an actual practice session devoted to pitching. Continue to stroke these short shots with minimal right-hand grip pressure and no grabbing. Stabilize the "slap" with a firm left hand and wrist. Gradually lengthen your swing until it is full, but always return to this "mini-swing" slapping drill if you ever again start to top shots.

Should this simple drill fail to cure your topping, I suggest you also apply the following corrections in the order they appear.

1. Play the ball opposite the inside edge of your left heel or within an area no more than two inches farther back (toward stance-center). Playing the ball too far back may lead to downward chopping, and playing it too far forward to upward lifting.

2. Experiment by standing farther and closer to the ball than seems normal. You may have been crowding it or reaching for it. Either extreme can lead to lifting and chopping.

3. Address the ball with both hands and forearms free of tension. Too much grip and arm tension at address can lead to lifting and chopping.

4. Stress a long, slow, wide backswing with plenty of time at the top to change directions. Again avoid grabbing with your right hand during the downswing.

Causes and cures for
Fat Shots

Fat shots are simply a result of striking the wrong ball first. Your clubhead digs into Mother Earth before it reaches that smaller ball with the dimples.

For experienced players, fat shots, like topped shots, attack only occasionally, but often disastrously. You may "sclaff" only once a round, but inevitably it will be on a crucial pitch shot over sand or water.

More often than not fat shots indicate one or both of two closely allied swing problems — poor timing, and/or poor weight-shifting. In both cases the swing radius formed by the left arm and clubshaft becomes lengthened and/or lowered before impact. The clubhead, slowed by the turf, either cuts under the ball or upwards towards it.

In the properly-timed downswing the left leg, side, arm and hand *pull* the clubshaft down and forward. The clubhead trails everything else until the last split-second when — if it's not over-controlled by too much grip pressure — it automatically lowers to ball level and squares to the target line. Fat shots occur when this process is reversed. When the clubhead out-races the left hand, arm, side and leg, it reaches ball level — and then the turf — too soon, prior to impact.

Fat shots occur when swing radius formed by the left arm and clubshaft is re-established prior to impact. Clubhead thus reaches ground level before it gets to the ball and is slowed by the intervening turf.

Lee Trevino contacts ball and then the turf as is proper on iron shots. Fat shots occur when ball-turf sequence is reversed.

Proper weight-shifting onto the left foot at the start of the downswing helps establish proper timing, by forcing the clubhead into its proper role as a *trailer* in the downswing. Failure to shift to the left allows the right hand and arm to take over and throw the clubhead down and forward too soon — and thus into the ground. Actual falling back onto the right foot — reverse weight-shifting — not only accentuates this throwing action but also shifts the entire swing arc farther to your right so that the clubhead contacts the ground even farther behind the ball.

If poor weight-shifting and poor timing are twin causes of sclaffing, the obvious solution to the problem lies in learning to establish your left leg, side, arm and hand as leaders, and the clubhead as the trailer, in your downswing. To do this we must once again return to the "mini-swing" as the best and quickest means of replacing swing faults with proper technique. Once again, we must *regress,* in a sense, in order to *progress.*

The anti-sclaffing drill begins with chipping short shots with a 7- or 8-iron. Make sure you have good turf so that the ball sets up nicely, because the better the lie the less you'll tend to throw the clubhead under the ball with your right hand in

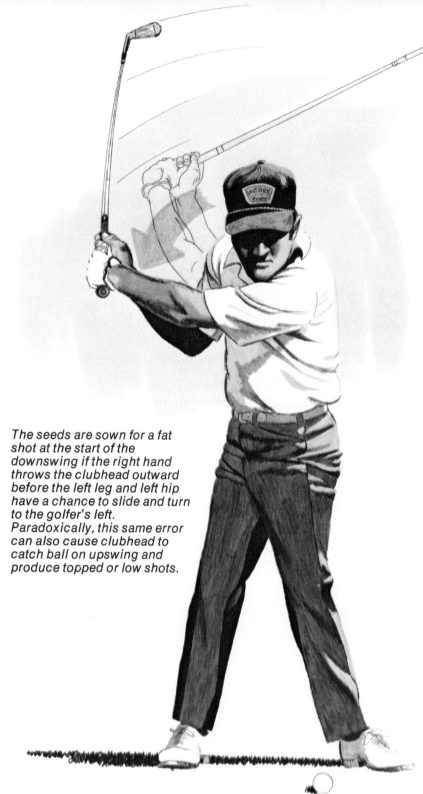

Lee Trevino's proper ball-turf contact shown on page 79 is set up by the way he starts his downswing. He gives himself sufficient time between backswing and downswing for his left knee to slide left instead of his right hand throwing clubhead outward, a move that can re-establish a full left arm-clubshaft radius prior to impact.

The seeds are sown for a fat shot at the start of the downswing if the right hand throws the clubhead outward before the left leg and left hip have a chance to slide and turn to the golfer's left. Paradoxically, this same error can also cause clubhead to catch ball on upswing and produce topped or low shots.

order to get it air-borne — a move that, in itself, leads to sclaffing.

The shot I want you to practice is one in which you make a short backswing with a very early wrist cock. Swing the clubhead back and up by relying almost solely on your left hand and wrist. This movement puts your left hand and arm so much in control that they must dominate your forward stroke. It also puts the clubhead in position to trail instead of lead into the ball.

Once you've made this short, left-hand-controlled backswing, merely slide your knees toward your target to start your forward swing. This move shifts your weight properly to the left and helps

you to pull, rather than throw, the clubhead back to the ball. Retain a sense of left-hand, left-wrist firmness as you swing your arms down and forward.

Practice this drill until you consistently contact the ball crisply — until it feels "light" when struck. Thereafter, gradually lengthen your swing, all the while retaining the feeling of left-hand control while leading the downswing with your knees.

This drill should quickly eliminate hitting fat. If, by chance, you should go to the other extreme and start topping the ball, merely lighten your grip pressure in both hands, throughout your swing, to allow a freer unhinging of your wrists. If you

should happen to continue sclaffing your shots, stick with the mini-swing drill I've described but also include the following modifications:

1. Address the ball with a bit more weight set on the inside of your *right* foot. This will give you a base from which to shift to the left on your forward swing.

2. Play the ball a shade farther back — to your right — in your stance.

3. Open your stance slightly and toe out your left foot to encourage leading with your knees.

4. Choke down on the clubshaft. This will reduce the need for you to rely on right-hand grip pressure during the swing.

Shanking occurs when the hosel rather than the clubface contacts the ball. This may result either from shoving the clubhead outward beyond the ball (top drawing), or extreme leading with the hosel ahead of the club's toe (bottom drawing), or from a combination of both.

Causes and cures for
Shanking

I know a fellow who suffered through a mind-blowing period of shanking when he was 13 years old. The problem started during a practice round for his state amateur tournament — his first tournament against adults — and stayed with him for about six weeks.

Seven years later this same golfer was playing a practice round for his college's conference tournament, which was to begin the next day. During that round he happened to shank his tee shot on one of the par-three holes.

Though he had conquered shanking long before and all but forgotten about the problem, this particular shot in this particular situation began to prey on this young man's mind. During the four rounds of tournament golf that followed, he shanked a total of four shots. Each occurred on the tee of that same par-three hole.

This man's experience shows how shanking, more than any other golfing problem — except perhaps "yipping" short putts — is a problem of the mind as much as the body. The longer shanking persists, the more mental and physical tension it creates. The more tense you become, the more you shank.

The first step in breaking this vicious cycle is to understand the enemy. Shanking is caused

Falling forward onto the toes (see drawing) is a common cause of shanking. Clubhead is shoved outward. Photo shows Lanny Wadkins approaching impact with clubhead well inside the target line. His weight has shifted onto his left heel as his left hip has cleared to his left.

by striking the ball with the hosel, or neck, of the club instead of the clubface. The ball shoots off to the right of your line at as much as 50-60 degrees to the actual target.

Basically, there are two ways to shank. The most common is to shove or push the clubhead out beyond the ball so that only the hosel is in position to make contact. The second way is to make contact with an extremely open clubface — so open that the heel leads the toe to such an extent that it alone can strike the ball. Frequently both problems combine, because shoving or pushing the clubhead outward with the right shoulder and/or the hands on the downswing involves grabbing the clubshaft with the hands, which prohibits free squaring of the clubface.

The best way to avoid shoving the clubhead outward from your body and beyond the ball is to eliminate the one thing that *must* anatomically accompany such shoving. That one thing is falling forward onto your toes. Remedy falling forward and you immediately eliminate the outward shoving that causes most shanking.

Falling forward often results from a player setting up at address with too much weight on his heels. Then, later during the downswing, centrifugal force pulls outward on the club and drags the player forward onto his toes.

Most of the better players I've observed address the ball with most of their weight on the balls of the feet, then during the swing shift it toward the heels, thereby offsetting the outward pull and routing the downswing path from well inside to along the target line at impact.

If you are shanking, I thus suggest that you first practice short shots with your weight consciously on the balls of your feet at address. Keep it there throughout your swing or, if possible, shift it toward your heels on your forward stroke. The big thing to avoid is falling forward onto your toes.

You'll find it easier to achieve proper weight distribution if you also try to route your clubhead straight back from the ball during your takeaway — from "three o'clock" if you can imagine the ball as being a clockface — and return it on your downswing from well inside the line, or from "four o'clock."

This drill may end your shanking, or it may be only a first step toward licking this often-persistent problem. If you still shank, here are some other ways to attack the dread disease:

1. Consciously strive for a longer, slower backswing with ample time at the top to change directions. Short, fast backswings lead to grabbing and pushing with the hands and shoving with the right shoulder at the start of the downswing.

2. Hold the club lightly at address and try to avoid grabbing it with your right hand during the backswing. Such grabbing creates right-side tension that cuts short your backswing and leads to outward shoving and pushing on the downswing.

3. Strive to turn your hips freely to the left during your downswing.

4. Consciously rotate the clubshaft to your left — counterclockwise — with your *left hand and forearm* during your downswing. Try to make the toe of the club catch up with, if not pass, the heel by impact.

Causes and cures for

Loss of Length

Good golfers pace their swings to drive the ball far. Notice how Bruce Crampton (above), Ben Crenshaw and Gary Player (pages 86-87) all set the club gently into position at the top of the backswing. They all take enough time to allow their legs and hips to start unwinding and lead the downswing. Meanwhile their hands and the club remain passively "quiet." There is no evidence of rushing the clubhead back to the ball, the fatal distance-robbing mistake that most golfers make when seeking additional length.

I see it happening every day I teach golf — pupils striving mightily to drive the ball farther and, in the end, making all the mistakes that actually rob them of distance.

There is no doubt in my mind that nine out of 10 players can definitely increase their distance, once they appreciate and experience just how little physical effort really is needed to drive a golf ball a long way. Let's face it: how much effort

should it take for a 150-*pound* man to swing a 14-*ounce* club against a highly resilient object weighing less than *two ounces?*

Distance comes from clubhead speed and square contact. Extreme physical effort to muscle the ball thwarts proper timing of the swing, which is the main factor in producing clubhead speed and square contact. Extreme physical effort also creates tension, and tension *always decreases*

clubhead speed and square contact. In short, what we need to drive a golf ball a long distance is not hippopotamus-like strength, but rather deer-like grace, motion and flexibility.

When most golfers seek distance, they instinctively rely on their upper bodies, especially their back and shoulder muscles. These are slow-moving parts, however. Excessive shoulder action reduces arm and hand speed, and therefore distance. Some golfers do turn to the hands and arms for added distance, but even these faster-moving parts can add clubhead speed only if applied at the proper time. Usually they are unleashed too early, with the result that, by impact, nothing is left to accelerate the clubhead through the ball. Increased hand and arm speed is a plus-factor in adding distance only if the player can move his legs and lower-body commensurately faster and thus preserve his timing.

In seeking extra distance I suggest you first reflect on the *pace* of your backswing. Most golfers have no concept of backswing pace. They swing back and up so fast that they inevitably lose some degree of control over the club. Then, instinctively they grab onto it tighter. Thereby they sacrifice freedom of motion, timing, balance, flexibility, clubhead control, and all the other things that contribute to striking a golf ball far. A fast backswing for a golfer seeking distance makes about as much sense as starting a car in heavy traffic and then jamming down on the accelerator.

Some people say that golfers, by and large, cannot reduce their "rational" (or instinctive) backswing pace. I say they can — and must. If you can't control your backswing, how in the world can you expect to control your forward swing. It's like learning penmanship: at first you simply cannot expect to write fast *and* legibly.

It is true that a few golfers with fast backswings do manage to drive the ball far. But how

many of us have Arnold Palmer's hand and arm strength? Better examples of proper backswing pace are such long drivers as Sam Snead, Jack Nicklaus, Johnny Miller, Ben Crenshaw, and countless others.

Let me emphasize, then, that if you need distance, you cannot make a free enough, smooth enough, slow enough, long enough *arm-swing* around your body. Such an arm-swing will automatically coil your body fully without conscious effort on your part.

Once you have learned to make this long, slow, smooth backswing, it is equally important that you start your downswing gently, quietly and effortlessly. At first a slower backswing will make you feel relatively powerless: all your instinctive urges will be to lash and lunge at the ball on the downswing. You must resist this temptation. Strive for a light, free and *gradual* acceleration of movement *through* impact. Sense that the ball is light and resilient, that it

merely happens to be in the way of your clubhead but offers no resistance to it whatsoever.

As you practice the kind of swing I've just described, do not worry at first about making square contact. You may make 50 such swings and only strike one or two shots square, but those one or two will tell you a great deal about your ability to generate extra length. Continued effort will gradually give you more distance more often. Your improvement will be even more rapid if you also:

1. Hold the club lightly, both at address and throughout your swing.

2. Learn to waggle the club and keep yourself in motion before starting your actual swing — in other words, don't freeze over the ball.

3. Maintain a steady head throughout your stroke.

Causes and cures for
High Shots

Most golfers worry only about distance and accuracy—seldom about trajectory. If a given drive flies straight and reasonably far, the average club player couldn't care less if it clotheslines out quail high or floats up and down like a mortar shot.

Only those golfers who are extremely knowledgeable and precise seem very concerned about how high a given shot flies (Ben Hogan was immensely particular in this area). Therefore, I congratulate readers seeking help in this section on avoiding high shots and/or the next section on doing away with those that fly too low.

Trajectory *is* important in golf. Extremely high shots, for instance, are especially vulnerable in gusty wind and therefore tough to judge in terms of both accuracy and distance. Also, shots that fly too high might easily have been "fat" shots, because the same problems that cause a player to fly a ball too high can very easily cause him to throw the clubhead into the ground behind it.

Ultra-high shots generally result from too much of the *wrong kind* of wrist action. There are two ways you can hinge and unhinge your wrists. Proper wrist action for golf is the type you get when you pound your fist on a tabletop. Try it with your left hand and you'll notice some hinging and unhinging at the base of your thumb. The back of your hand and forearm, however, remain in a constant relationship, more or less in a straight line.

High shots can result when the back of the left wrist breaks down and cups inward just before or during impact. This breakdown turns the clubface upward so that shots fly too high. More club control in the last three fingers of the left hand, and/or less right-hand throwing, will eliminate this left wrist breakdown.

Johnny Miller retains firm left-hand control of clubshaft through impact (note straight-line relationship between back of left hand, wrist and lower forearm) and thus contacts ball with clubface carrying its normal degree of loft.

This is the type of wrist action that, during the latter stages of the downswing, lowers the clubhead to the ball as your hands and arms swing forward and gradually turn the clubface toward the target. If the back of your left wrist remains fairly straight and firm through impact, and if your arms and hands turn back to more or less their original address position, your clubface will arrive at the ball carrying its normal loft. Assuming the ball is also squarely struck, the shot will then fly at a normal height.

Incorrect wrist action is the type you'd get if you flicked an ant off the top of the table with the back of your fingers. Notice how this kind of flicking motion causes the *back* of your wrist to bend inward, breaking the straight line between the back of your hand and forearm. When such inward bending at the back of the left wrist occurs near impact in your golf swing, the clubface must turn upward slightly as it comes into the ball, so that, even when you make solid contact, the extra loft causes the shot to fly higher than normal.

Inward collapsing of the left wrist is a common handicap-golfer's fault, indicating too little control of the clubshaft with the last three fingers of the left hand. It means that you need firmer left-hand, left-wrist control *throughout* your swing; or, conversely, *less* throwing action with your right hand, which is the main cause of left-wrist breakdown.

The best way I know to build left-hand control is through a simple drill that I call "hit and hold." Start with chip shots. Strike each ball with normal hand-arm acceleration on your forward stroke, but cut off your clubhead's movement as soon as you possibly can *after* it contacts the ball. You'll find this holding action demands maximum clubshaft control in the last three fingers of your left hand. Without good left-hand control, the back of your wrist will cup inward and your clubhead will continue moving forward and up.

It may take several practice sessions but you should stick with this drill until you can finish your stroke with the back of your left hand, wrist and forearm still in a straight line. Once you can do this on chip shots, gradually working the same left-hand control into your full swing will enable you to make crisper shots with all your clubs as well as flying shots on a normal trajectory. Also, you'll begin to pinch the ball solidly against the turf with your irons instead of scuffing underneath or blading into the back of it.

If you should find it difficult to hold the back of your left wrist firm through impact and into your follow-through, I suggest you also:

1. Think in terms of swinging *through* the ball, not *at* it. Swinging *at* instead of *through* the ball makes you unconsciously decelerate your hands' forward swinging motion, which in turn forces the back of your left wrist to break down as the clubhead continues forward and up.

2. Try to maintain a consistently light right-hand grip pressure through the swing.

3. Concentrate on shifting your left knee to the left at the very start of the downswing.

4. Hold the club slightly more in the palm, and less in the fingers, of your left hand.

Miller demonstrates perfect wrist action in his golf swing. Notice that his left wrist hinges and unhinges freely at the base of his thumb, but that the back of his left hand, wrist and forearm remain perfectly straight throughout, indicating firm left-hand control.

Causes and cures for
Low Shots

Proper address position helps produce shots of normal trajectory. Note how Tommy Bolt sets up with his right shoulder, hip and knee slightly lower than their left-side counterparts. His right leg is flexed inward slightly and his head is over his right knee. More of his weight sets on the inside of his right foot than on his left.

For your shots to fly at a reasonable height, three conditions must be met when the ball leaves the clubhead. These conditions concern clubface loft, backspin, and forward thrust. If your shots fly too low, one or more of these factors is at least partially out of whack.

Let's first talk about clubface loft. We'll assume that your driver, for instance, carries about the standard 11 degrees of loft. If, during impact, your hands and clubhead are properly related — the line formed by your left arm and clubshaft is straight — your clubface should still be carrying 11 degrees of loft, and your shot should *leave* the clubface on a trajectory of, again, about 11 degrees.

However, if your hands are *too far ahead of your clubhead* at impact, your clubface loft will be, in effect, less than normal — perhaps only as much as eight or nine degrees. Naturally, it will then drive the ball forward at this lower angle. (Expert golfers purposely strive for this hands-leading-clubhead effect when they are trying to punch a low shot, say under a tree limb. They merely play the ball farther back in their stance, which sets it, in effect, behind their hands at both address and impact.)

While clubface loft at impact largely determines the shot's *initial* takeoff angle, the factors that determine whether or not it continues rising and how high it eventually flies are backspin and forward thrust. The more backspin and forward thrust the ball carries, the higher and farther it will fly. The amount of each is determined largely by clubhead speed and the angle at which the clubhead approaches the ball. For example, your shots will lack forward thrust if your clubhead speed is slow, or if the angle of the clubhead's delivery to the ball is too sharply downward instead of

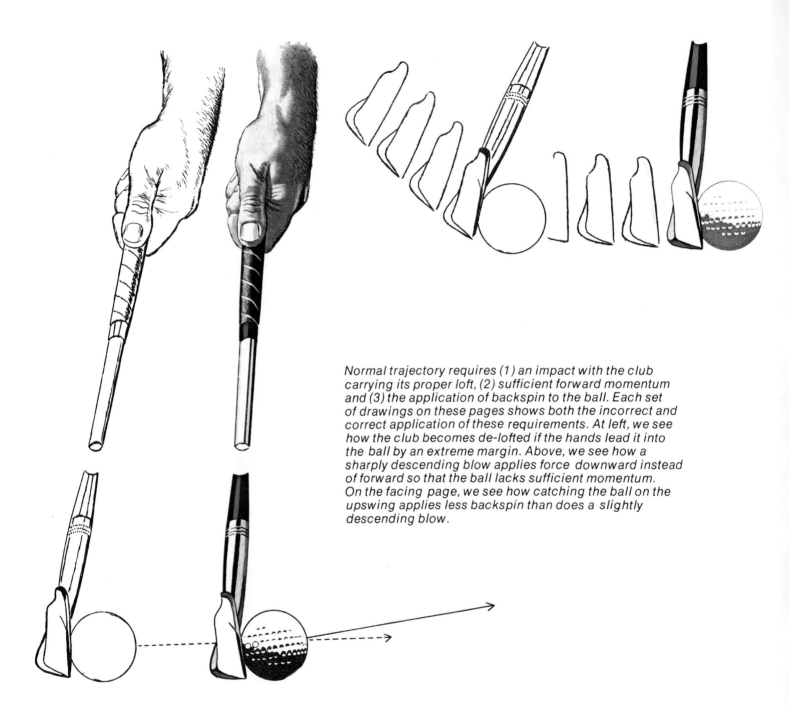

Normal trajectory requires (1) an impact with the club carrying its proper loft, (2) sufficient forward momentum and (3) the application of backspin to the ball. Each set of drawings on these pages shows both the incorrect and correct application of these requirements. At left, we see how the club becomes de-lofted if the hands lead it into the ball by an extreme margin. Above, we see how a sharply descending blow applies force downward instead of forward so that the ball lacks sufficient momentum. On the facing page, we see how catching the ball on the upswing applies less backspin than does a slightly descending blow.

forward, or both combined. In the same way, you will lack backspin if your clubhead speed is low, or if your clubhead is moving *upward* during impact, or both. Thus, to summarize, you may be hitting your shots too low because during impact:

1. Your hands are so far in front of the clubhead that you've reduced your clubface loft, and/or . . .

2. Your shot lacks sufficient *forward* thrust because your clubhead is moving too sharply *downward* and/or lacks enough speed, or . . .

3. Your clubhead is catching the ball on your upswing and thus minimizing the amount of backspin you impart to it.

Because so many different impact situations can cause a low shot, there are several ways to alleviate or cure the problem. One of the best I know is to modify your address position as follows:

Set up to the ball with your left side higher and your right side lower than normal, with your right shoulder, hip and knee noticeably lower than your left shoulder, hip and knee. To make this adjustment correctly, you will need to flex your right knee inward slightly, towards your left leg, and slide your head a bit to your right, so that it sets more or less over your right knee.

The thing to avoid in setting up this way is turning your body to your left as you flex your right knee inward. Such turning could set your body too "open," aligned too far left of target.

The quickest way to habitualize this new address position is to strike a few batches of practice shots from a slightly uphill slope, say about 15 degrees, which is more or less equivalent to the takeoff trajectory of a normal three-wood shot. Practicing from such a slope automatically sets you into the address position I've described. Once you sense how this position feels, and can duplicate it on level ground, you should find that your shots fly higher. If your shots are still too low for your liking, I suggest you also do one or more of the following:

1. Play the ball either farther forward or farther back in your stance. Experiment with the positioning to find the adjustment you need. You may have been catching shots on the upswing — applying too little backspin — because of playing the ball too far forward; or too early in your downswing — attacking it at too steep an angle — because of its being too far back.

2. Make sure you turn your right side to your right on your backswing to avoid merely lifting the club up and back with your hands and arms.

3. Hold the club a bit more in the fingers and less in the palm of your left hand, especially if your low shots also have been curving from left to right.

Causes and cures for
Inconsistency

It's expensive to have even one repeatedly bad shot that clutters up your game. Yet, even if you slice constantly, say, you still at least know your enemy, and are thereby able either to take specific corrective steps, or simply allow for your shots to bend from left to right. The same is true of pulling or hooking, and, while it is difficult to allow for a topped or fat shot, or a shank, in each case you do at least have a well-defined problem and specific medicine to cope with it.

The truly unfortunate golfer is the one who, say, slices his drive, hooks his second shot, tops his third, sclaffs his approach into sand, shanks his first bunker shot, and then three-putts when he eventually gets to the green. This sort of general inconsistency is like having a backache that defies correct diagnosis. Take two aspirin — or a big drink — and go to bed!

General inconsistency of shotmaking can result from excessive head movement. The photos here and on the facing page show Sam Snead's steady head from the start of his swing through impact. While his head does turn with his shoulders, a comparison of its positioning with the trees in the background reveals little or no up-down movement or sideways swaying.

Many golfers who suffer from general inconsistency have one *basic* error that triggers most of their other errors. A mistake at address leads to several different mistakes during the swing which produce a wide variety of bad shots. Or the 57 varieties of mishits can result from a player's constant experimentation — a new gimmick on almost every swing — as he searches for the panacea to his basic, but unknown, problem. Also, there are times when the body reacts subconsciously during the swing to correct an earlier error. When it happens to over-react, the result is still another way of visiting the jungle.

When your game reaches the point where you have absolutely no clue as to just how you're going to mess up your next shot, I must tell you quite honestly that it's time to see a competent teaching professional, instead of

trying to find a cure-all in books or magazines (even those written by Bob Toski). Only someone watching you actually swing can determine exactly what your particular *basic* problem is, and then decide which basic corrective medicine is best for you.

If you should run into a mixture of bad shots during a round, however, with no expert help readily available, here are a few "Band Aids" to help hold your game more or less together:

1. Hold the club lighter at address and throughout your swing. Bad shots cause tension and, thus, more bad shots. A lighter grip will almost always help break this cycle.

2. Slow your backswing. A main cause of bad shots is a faster swing than you normally use. Previous bad shots can trigger the faster swing. So can a lack of confidence in yourself or your game. Whatever the cause, a slower backswing will help to give you the few good shots you need to get back on track both mentally and physically.

3. Make a conscious effort to swing with a steady head. Swaying, either side-to-side or up-down, makes solid contact difficult if not impossible. Also, the bad shots that result can lead to even more experimentation and thus to an even wider spectrum of errors.

4. Use more club on approach shots, while also trying to hit your drives 20 yards shorter than normal. These gimmicks will vastly improve the pace of your swing and thus help you avoid tension, poor timing, and swaying.

Beyond these suggestions, perhaps the best way to break a string of bad shots during play is simply to "think target." Too often we select a target, aim more or less towards it, and then switch our minds from it to various swing thoughts. Thus we give our subconscious mind a confusing variety of orders, which leads to a wide variety of bad shots.

Your subconscious will trigger many good moves as you swing — it will actually correct earlier mistakes — but only if you give it a clear image of precisely what you are trying to accomplish. We call this use of imagery in golf "target projection."

The technique is quite similar to that which you have used in your home or office when going from one room to the next in the dark. Before switching out the light in one room you focus your attention on the doorknob to the next room. You try to sense how it will feel to walk to it in the dark. After you switch off the light, you retain the image of the doorknob in your mind's eye as you walk to it. Given free rein, your subconscious will take you to it almost every time.

In golf we merely substitute our target for the doorknob. Then we sense how our swing should feel and how the shot should look. Finally, we "see" the target — just as we imagined the doorknob — as we address the ball and swing.

The more you apply target projection as you practice and play golf, the easier it will become for you to keep your target in mind as you swing. Thereby you will gradually transfer a clearer image of what you are trying to do to your subconscious. It, in turn, will then do a better job of directing your anatomy in producing the shot you have in mind.

Shots become more consistent as you develop the ability to retain the image of your target in your mind's eye while swinging. A good way to develop this knack is to practice pitch or chip shots by sighting the target and then retaining its image while swinging with your eyes closed.

Bad putting can start with carelessness, such as one-handing and missing a short putt (left-hand figure). This leads to tension and anguish that causes similar missing even when the player is methodical about his execution (center figure). Soon the player actually anticipates missing (right-hand figure) which creates still greater tension, over-concern about technique and continual experimentation. A proper attitude is to plan and execute putts with care, but without over-concern about missing.

George Archer successfully applies the mechanical suggestions mentioned in the text. Note at left the positioning of the ball under his eyes, and the high position of his hands. In the sequence above, note the free swinging of the arms back and forward, a result, no doubt, of a constantly light grip pressure throughout.

Causes and cures for
Bad Putting

If poor putting is pushing your scores up and dragging the rest of your game and your psyche down, you should first take an honest look at the problem as it applies to you in particular. Ask yourself candidly if, perhaps, the cause of your trouble might not be mental as well as physical — and answer yourself honestly. A bad *attitude* toward putting often leads to a poor putting stroke. In such cases, it obviously makes sense to change your attitude before altering your technique.

Regarding attitude, either one of two extremes can bring you trouble. The first extreme is sheer carelessness. Sooner or later careless putting leads to a day or two of really *bad* putting, which then leads to the other extreme, an overconcern about missing putts. Naturally, other pressure-producing factors, such

as a match for unusually high stakes, can also cause a fear of missing.

Once you begin to worry about missing putts, you begin to generate tension that causes more missing. Fear of missing also leads to overconcern about technique. Once into this vicious circle, you change your style from day to day, grasping at gimmicks that are seldom lasting, and your stroke becomes too mechanical, too over-controlled. Thus the problem snowballs endlessly, with tension producing bad technique, and bad technique causing even more missed putts that lead to even more tension.

The first step toward recovery is to develop an attitude about putting that falls somewhere between the extremes of carelessness and over-concern about missing. Try to make *all* putts, but go about doing so with the awareness that a miss adds only one stroke to your score. It won't, in itself, ruin your round — or your life — unless you let it.

Down through the years, the games's best putters — Walter Hagen, Bobby Jones, Horton Smith, Bobby Locke, Billy Casper — were inevitably players who each found a method that worked well for him, developed it through constant practice, stuck with it through hot and cold streaks, and, above all, accepted the fact that he was human enough to make a poor putt from time to time.

Once you adopt such an approach, you should then go about building "success patterns," by re-establishing your confidence through consistently sinking putts of gradually increasing length. Start with short putts, say two-footers, and don't move farther away until you meet whatever standard you wish to set for yourself — 9 out of 10, 10 of 20, 20 of 20, 50 of 50, or whatever.

While much of putting technique is up to the personal preference of the individual, there are certain basics that I would encourage any golfer — especially if he or she is struggling — to at least consider trying. If you should choose to incorporate any of these basics, be sure that you do so on *every* putt, even the two-footers:

1. Always "see" the putt running up to and into the hole *before* you actually make your stroke. At first this image of a successful putt may be fuzzy, but in time and with practice the picture that you transfer to your subconscious mind will sharpen. The sharper the image, the better job your subconscious will do in helping you to make the stroke you need to hole the putt. This technique of "target projection" is especially vital if you often think about missing putts as you are addressing the ball, or if you tend to change your mind about distance or direction during the stroke, or if at times you seem to have little or no sense of touch.

2. Hold the putter as lightly as you can at address. Avoid any sudden increase of grip pressure during the stroke. The lighter your grip, the better your sense of feel for the rhythm of the moving putterhead.

3. Address the ball with your hands "high." The grip end of your putter should run up the channel of your left hand, between the thumb and heel pads, rather than under the heel pad as on full shots. The higher hand position will keep your putterhead swinging back and forward along the target line longer. It will also force you to make a freer, more pendulum-like, arm-stroke if you now happen to be overly-wristy in your stroke.

4. Play the ball just far enough from your toes so that when you bend forward to a comfortable position over the ball, your eyes are directly over the target line, not out beyond nor inside it.

5. Work on the pace and timing of your stroke until it becomes free and unhurried. Learn to smoothly and gradually *accelerate* your arms forward through contact, without grabbing or shoving the club with your hands.

6. Practice your putting until all "mechanics" of set-up and stroking become second-nature; until your putting is nothing more than (1) planning, (2) "seeing" a successful putt, and (3) stroking solely through a sense of "touch" or "feel" for the moving putterhead.

PART 3: SWING MODELS TO KEEP IN MIND

"There is much to be learned from the swings of our best players, especially when we know what to study about their technique. Equally valuable, however, is the overall feeling one gets from looking at good swings. It is this general feeling for a good swing that amateur golfers should strive to summon forth within themselves as they prepare for, and actually play, their shots on the course."

— Bob Toski

Here we see the most successful golfer in history making two swings with his driver. In each case Jack Nicklaus was trying to fade the ball slightly from left to right—his favorite shape of shot with this club—toward the tree shown on the far right of the pictures in the second swing series.

Jack hit both drives about 270 yards. Both finished on target. The second drive shown did fade as he had planned. The first did not—it flew straight—but I'm sure that he found the result more than acceptable.

His first shot did not fade because his leg and hip action during his downswing was a bit slower than he had intended. Thus his arms turned the clubface back to an on-target facing at impact, rather than the slightly open facing that he had hoped to achieve.

Beyond this slight mis-timing of his downswing and, on both shots, a barely noticeable lifting of his head during the backswing, Jack's technique as shown here clearly portrays each of the fundamentals that I have discussed in the first section of this book. I suggest that the reader review those fundamentals briefly and then study Jack's technique closely. I can think of no better way to develop a clear mental image of the fundamentals that I stress.

Some of the things that I especially admire in Jack's swing are:

—The way he sets his head well behind the ball, to the right of it, at address.

—The way he lets his hips and shoulders turn fully during his backswing as a **result** of his arms and the club swinging freely.

—The overall width of his backswing, a direct result of his left hand and arm controlling the club, as well as his starting the clubhead back along—not inside—the target line.

—His setting of the clubshaft on a line parallel to his target line at the top of his backswing **(No. 5 photo, second swing)**.

—His passive hands and wrists at the start of his downswing. Jack's right hand doesn't throw the club outward, but rather his arms swing it downward and forward freely from well inside the target line. His legs lead; his shoulders follow.

—The way he continues to look at the ball with his **left** eye throughout his downswing. This helps assure that his clubhead will approach the ball on a level path from inside to along his intended line.

—The free, uninhibited swinging of his arms through impact and beyond. His left arm swishes forward, leading the way, never slowing down to allow his right hand a chance to close the clubface to the left or flip the clubhead upward.

Unfortunately, there are certain important reasons for Jack's success that no sequence of swing photos could possibly show:

—The disciplined pace of his swing—no rushing whatsoever.

—The disciplined mental approach—no shot is more important than the one at hand.

—The absolute dedication to fundamentals—no swing alteration is worth trying if it doesn't apply directly to a basic fundamental.

—The unwillingness to ever make a careless or purposeless swing, even in practice.

Thus the Nicklaus swing is one that any and all golfers should study not only for what it shows, but also for what it implies.

BEN CRENSHAW

Here is a young man with a very good—though not flawless—golf swing. He hits an unusually long ball and putts superbly. And he wins. That's what really matters.

There is much to be said for Ben's technique as shown here on two different drives.

In the address position photos, I particularly like the way his arms hang freely, apparently without tension. His right hand seems to be caressing the club. I believe that most golfers could improve their swings straightaway if they would merely hold the club lightly in this hand, both at address and throughout the swing.

You will also notice that Ben, like Jack Nicklaus, starts with his head well behind the ball. Though it rotates with the swinging of his arms, it never moves up, down or sideways.

Also like Nicklaus, Ben makes a wide and full backswing. Again, this indicates a relaxed right hand and arm, free of tension that might otherwise inhibit his left arm from fully extending and freely swinging the club.

If there is one aspect of Ben's swing that I find less than ideal, it is the path of his backswing in the early stage. I hope he won't mind my spotlighting this seemingly minor flaw, to show readers how one basic imperfection can lead to a series of swing compensations. Ben obviously makes these adjustments successfully, but most golfers—lacking his talent—do not.

It seems to me that in the second swing series **(photos 3 and 4)** he has swung the club a bit more around and behind himself—to the "inside"— that I consider ideal. I say this because many golfers who swing the club well inside the target line so early in the backswing react by looping it in the opposite direction—toward the outside— early in the downswing. This outward looping causes the clubhead to approach the ball steeply

downward and from slightly outside the target line. A low pull-slice that flies from left to right is the most common result.

Ben avoids the loop to the outside because he drives his legs and hips laterally—sideways—to the left at the start of his downswing turn. This pulls the club downward **from** the inside before it can start moving **to** the outside. Also, his swing is so well-paced and rhythmical that he allows himself sufficient time between backswing and downswing to start this lateral shifting.

Now, while **some** lateral movement of the hips and knees is desirable at the start of the downswing, an extreme sideways slide makes it very difficult to turn the left hip sufficiently to the left. This turning to the left is necessary to allow the left arm a clear path to accelerate freely forward.

Ben helps himself clear his hips somewhat by the way he replants his left heel at the start of his downswing. He sets it down in a way that leaves his left foot toed out well to the left.

Yet even this compensation doesn't appear quite sufficient to allow his left hip to clear fully. Photo No. 10 in the first series shows that his left leg has been forced to stiffen just before impact, and thus lengthen sufficiently to allow room for his arms and the club to swing forward without scuffing the shot.

Without his excellent left-hand control, this left-leg stiffening would probably allow his right hand to misalign the clubface, causing his shots to frequently fly off line.

In short, I feel that Ben could avoid the need for these swing compensations if he would, at the start of his backswing, simply swing the clubhead back from the ball **along** his target line for at least a few inches, thus reducing slightly the amount that his hands move around and behind his body.

GARY PLAYER

Those who argue that golf is not an athletic game should study these photos of Gary Player. Given the swing technique that he has developed, only a person with a unique blend of strength, suppleness, coordination and sensitive rhythm could even begin to approach the success of this great champion.

Gary addresses the ball from a static position—no clubhead waggling—and with a degree of arm tension that would stifle most golf swings from the start. Usually this much arm tension restricts the length, fluidity and rhythm of the swing by making a player rely on his shoulders and upper body to move the club, causing him to jerk it back and then shove it forward on a steeply downward, outside-to-inside, clubhead path. The shot is usually a low and weak slice from left to right or, sometimes, a straight pull to the left.

Gary then turns his clubhead open to the right very early in his backswing **(first series, Photo No. 2)**. As it does in Gary's case, such independent turning of the hands and arms frequently produces a fairly "flat" backswing.

Thus at the top of Gary's backswing **(second series, Photo No. 5)** we see that a line along his left arm and another across his shoulders would form almost identical planes. Such similarity also tends to make most golfers lunge at the ball with their shoulders. Ideally the arm plane should be a bit more upright than the shoulder plane at this point, so that the arms can swing somewhat independently of the shoulders, moving freely downward and forward.

Gary, however, brilliantly overcomes these seemingly troublesome tendencies. First, he breaks down his address position tension with a fairly dramatic "forward press," consisting of a kick of the right knee and a movement of his hands to the left just before beginning his backswing. It appears that Photo No. 1 of the first series was taken during this forward press.

Next, Gary's amazing suppleness allows him to make a full arm swing and, as a result, a full shoulder turn during his backswing, all while barely turning his hips. The vast difference between the degree of his shoulder and hip turns creates tremendous potential leverage that, if correctly applied, can result in extremely long shots.

Gary applies this energy correctly by starting his downswing with his legs and arms, rather than his shoulders. His knees drive forward as his hips turn to the left. His arms start moving the club downward and forward **before** his shoulders have a chance to shove it outward. As a result, his clubhead approaches the ball from well inside his target line, which allows his clubhead to move into the ball on a fairly shallow angle of attack, thus applying the force of the blow forward instead of downward.

While Gary's occasional bad shot is, in fact, a sharp hook to the left, he generally avoids this problem by doing three things that all golfers should strive to accomplish.

First, again because of his suppleness, he manages to turn and clear his left hip out of the way while driving his knees laterally to the left. Without this turning he would block his shots out to the right or quickly close the clubface to the left through impact.

Second, he never lets his left arm decelerate into and through impact. The left arm should pace your golf swing, both back and forward. When it slows down, the hands take over, flip the clubhead upward and misalign the clubface.

Third, Gary holds the clubface on a line into and through impact with firm left-hand control. He never lets his right hand outrace his left, but rather allows the clubface to square itself as a result of swinging his arms freely down and forward.

ARNOLD PALMER

Arnold Palmer is another example of a golfer who has achieved greatness with a swing that, like Lee Trevino's, is somewhat unorthodox.

Arnold sets up farther than normal from the ball, reaching for it with his hands relatively far away from his body. We shall later see how this departure from the normal address position greatly affects his swing.

Arnold also addresses the ball with his head in a slightly unorthodox position. He points his chin at the ball, rather than well behind it as does, say, Jack Nicklaus. Thus Arnold must turn his head slightly counterclockwise during his backswing to reach the same point that others achieve at address.

I like the way Arnold holds the club, with the back of his left hand more or less facing the target. I also like the way he sets his right shoulder, hip and knee lower than their left-side counterparts. With his right knee tucked inward slightly Palmer has set himself up with a nice, soft right side, ready to submit to left-side control throughout the swing.

I also like the fact that Arnold plays the ball forward in his stance, opposite his left heel. This forward positioning induces proper leg action in the downswing so that the lower-body and left side will pull the arms and clubshaft through the impact area.

Arnold's takeaway finds the clubhead moving straight back from the ball. It doesn't move inside the target line until it passes his right foot. Note the unified action of the hands, arms and shoulders. There is no forced action of the shoulders to turn too fast and become over-active during the backswing.

Though Arnold's clubhead starts straight back, it does move to the inside rather rapidly, as a result of his standing so far from the ball. In frames #3 and #4 on the next pages you'll also note a tendency for Arnold's right leg to straighten quickly. This, too, is a normal reaction to reaching for the ball at address, and of shifting the left knee toward it early in the backswing.

At the top of his backswing Arnold has excellent left-arm extension and a full shoulder turn, but it appears that some of his weight has shifted onto his left side, and that his right leg has almost straightened completely. From this position most golfers would spin quickly to the left on the downswing and throw the clubhead outside the line as their right hand, arm and shoulder outraced their left. They would find it difficult to lead the downswing with the legs thrusting laterally to the left.

Arnold manages to produce good leg and lower-body movement and thus pull the club down into position with his left arm and side in control. However, his swing does evidence more turning and less lateral sliding than, say, Lee Trevino's action.

During the downswing Arnold retains the cocked-wrist position common to all the great strikers of the ball, who combine this late-release position with the ability to deliver the clubhead freely and squarely at impact.

At impact Arnold's strong left arm and hand are still mastering the movement of the right, but shortly thereafter the cross-over of the hands is very apparent. Again, this is a result of the fact that he reaches for the ball. The wide angle in which he swings the club around his body forces the earlier cross-over.

The tremendously high finish Arnold makes, with his left arm carrying the clubface well over his head, is further indication that his strong left arm has really mastered that of his right arm and hand throughout his swing.

SAM SNEAD

Samuel Jackson Snead has played golf longer, better than anyone else in the history of the game. At 64 he seems to be striking the ball and competing almost as well as at any time during his 37-year career as a playing professional.

Sam is double-jointed and supple, and still in magnificent physical condition. He has the greatest golf swing I have ever seen in regard to sound fundamentals, tempo, rhythm, balance and timing. These assets, along with his love of the game, no doubt account for his longevity.

Sam's address position in the first frames on the following pages is something to behold. His left arm and clubshaft extend into almost one continuous line. His head is turned slightly to his right. His right side is passive and relaxed, ready to allow his left arm and side to master the movement of the clubhead around and over his body.

Sam starts his swing with a slight forward press of his knees and hands just prior to his takeaway. Like all great strikers of the ball, he displays excellent mobility and rhythm with the lower part of his body before starting back. He's always in motion.

In frames #2 we see that the clubhead swings relatively straight back from the ball before turning to the inside, a key characteristic of the modern swing. When the clubhead finally moves inside, it does so without any apparent turning of the wrists. The left arm is in complete control at this point.

Throughout his backswing Sam's left knee gradually turns to point behind the ball and his left heel lifts gradually but only slightly, even in this driver swing. Sam's right knee straightens slightly, but never completely. His legs, as well as his shoulders, are merely reacting to the swinging of the club with the arms: the arms are the leaders in the correct backswing. Though Sam's upper body coils fully in response to the movement of the club, his head remains in a fixed position. At the top of his backswing, Sam's driver reaches a position that is parallel with the ground and pointing at the target. If I had to recommend a specific top-of-the-swing position, this would be it. Sam has merely set the club into a place from which he can shift direction with his legs and lower body and readily swing the clubhead back to the ball from well inside to along the target line.

We see this shifting of the legs starting in frames #6 as the knees drive forward and force the left forearm and hand to pull the right forearm and hand down into proper position. In later frames you can see how fast Sam's hands and wrists react from the late-hit position and square the clubface against the ball. This reaction takes place automatically as a result of Snead making a proper backswing and pulling the club into position with his legs and left side early in his downswing. Through impact he's merely holding on to the speeding club with his hands, allowing centrifugal force to take him off his right side and around and up into a high finish. If you will note the wrinkling of Sam's sweater in the final frames, you'll sense just how much his forearms and hands pull his shoulder muscles around so that he finishes with almost all of his weight on his left side. To the end, his shoulders have followed, rather than led, the free-swinging of the clubshaft with his arms.

JOHNNY MILLER

While Johnny Miller is already one of the best players on the pro tour, I believe he has yet to realize his full potential. He's strong, tall, supple, has an excellent swing, a fine temperament and a lot of dedication—all it takes to reach the top.

In frames #1 on the following pages you'll notice that Miller plays the ball just off the instep of the left heel on this 6-iron shot. Johnny, being quite tall, sets his body posture more erect than most, but his arms and hands hang naturally from his shoulders. Again the right arm is passive, bent more than the left, which is thus in the commanding position. Johnny's head position is excellent, turned slightly to the right. Both knees are flexed and his body is aligned square to the target line.

During Miller's takeaway in frames #2, his left arm and hand are still very much in control. The back three fingers of his left hand are maintaining such mastery of the clubhead moving back that it looks as though he is actually pushing the left hand against the right, and thus avoiding the right hand turning the club away from the ball too quickly. In frames #3, his forearms and hands are moving inward and beginning to move upward. His hips and shoulders are coiling in sequence with the movement of his forearms and hands, and his right knee is beginning to straighten to some degree. His head remains steady in an excellent position over the ball.

In frames #4, John is really beginning to coil the upper part of his body and let the force of the winding action of the arms and hands set the club in position. In frames #5 you can see the complete coiling action of his hips and shoulders with the arms and hands swinging the club high over his right shoulder and creating a tremendous amount of leverage to start down into the ball.

You see the change of direction in frames #6: the crucial part of the swing from the top where the weight-shift begins to take place. Notice the lateral driving of the knees and the turning of the hips first toward the target and then to the left. Again, the important thing to observe here is how the left arm is being pulled down in position, with the right hand following and the shoulders reacting last of all.

John's weight shift is very apparent in frames #7 where the knees have become very active in driving to and through the ball. You also can see the strength of the left forearm muscles and left hand really in control, pulling hard to the left and leading the right hand into position.

A characteristic of most top modern-day golfers is that the left knee stays flexed in the hitting area much longer than ever before in the history of the game. This helps keep the left hand and left forearm in command through impact. Even though the right hand eventually begins to catch up to the left, the strength of the left forearm and hand force the right to stay well inside the line and close to the body.

In frames #8, the right-hand finally squares up the clubface. Here Johnny's body tilt is such that the right knee is really kicking in towards the left and his head has moved slightly down and back as a result. Eventually you can see the starting of the crossing over of the right hand, but the ball is now well on its way.

Miller's finish is one of the prettiest I've seen in golf, his hands finishing high over his left shoulder with his right arm extended and his weight well onto his left side.

LEE TREVINO

Lee Trevino has a very unique swing, one of the most unusual I've seen in a championship player. He seems to aim left and swing to the right, yet strikes the ball more or less straight toward the target. It's a highly effective technique, however, because he controls it well and because he has used it for many years and can trust it totally today. In golf you can have the finest style in the world but if you don't trust it, you won't win.

The important thing in golf is to first aim the club down the target line and then swing it on that line through impact. In frames #1 on the following pages we see that Lee aims slightly left with an open body position at address and with the ball well forward in his stance. However, his left arm is extended and his right arm slightly bent, so that his right side is passive and ready to submit to the stronger left side. Thus he is in position to start the clubhead away pretty much straight back from the ball, along the target line. In frames #2 look at the position of the lower part of Lee's body. He seems to have hardly moved at all from his waist down. He looks completely flat-footed. While the clubhead is finally beginning to move slightly inside the target line, he shows no apparent effort to try to turn his wrists very early in the backswing.

In frames #3 we see the arms swinging to the inside. It is very evident that Lee's right arm here is working passively: it is beginning to fold at the wrist and elbow as his left side remains extended. He seems to simply cock his right wrist and set the angle between his left arm and the clubshaft very early, a move that further subordinates the right arm so that it won't be used to lift the club going back and thereby throw or shove it back to the ball on the downswing.

In frames #4 you can see Trevino has not swung the club anywhere near to horizontal. His left heel, by remaining close to the ground, will not permit him to overswing, unless he were to bend his left arm.

Frames #5 are interesting in that we can see the apparent weight-shift to Lee's left taking place. It's apparent why Trevino says, "If I don't use my legs, I can't play." The lateral thrusting of his legs to the left allows him to maintain strong control of the club with his left hand and left arm. This left-side control is vital, because the swing plane of the club has produced a slight degree of shutness to the clubface. This forces Lee, as he moves into the downswing in frames #6, #7 and #8, to keep his left arm controlling and pulling the club shaft so that it doesn't turn over too early. Without left-side control, his right side would swing over and out and he'd hit the ball dead left.

The most unique feature of Trevino's swing is seen near the impact area in frames #9 and #10. Note how long he extends through the ball with his forearms and hands, the left hand not turning nearly as early as in the case of most tour players. Because the clubface is moving into the ball in a shut position, Lee must move laterally longer through the ball with his knees, with his arms staying extended and pulling the clubhead through the ball with his left forearm and hand. Though in frames #11 you can just begin to see the slight crossing of Lee's right hand over his left, the ball is, of course, well on its way towards the target by now.

Thus in frames #12 you'll note that Lee's hands are just slightly higher than his head. His body weight has moved well onto his left side but his arms and hands are beginning to extend around and up.

Most of the great modern players are strongly left-sided in the way they shift or slide the lower part of the body to the left early in the downswing. Their legs thrust laterally and then their hips turn to the left. This sliding and turning forces the forearms to react and accelerate the clubhead through the impact area. Trevino is an unusually strong left-sided player, and a great one because of his outstanding rhythm, his strong leg movement, his good balance and his ability to restrain the entire upper part of his body so that it follows the lead of his legs.

TOM WEISKOPF

The big thing to notice in Tom Weiskopf's excellent swing is how well he moves his legs and lower body as he changes direction at the top of the backswing. Like all great strikers of the ball, Tom uses his legs as leaders to pull the shoulders into position during the downswing. The average player leads his downswing with his shoulders turning to the left and strikes too early with his hands and wrists. He lacks the proper leg action that is needed to subordinate the shoulders.

I think Tom's address position is excellent. His left arm is extended and his right shoulder is slightly lower than his left. His hands are well placed on the club, with the back of the left hand facing the target.

In the frames #2 on the following pages, we see that Tom takes the club away from the ball with a unified action, typical of all the great modern strikers of the ball. Obviously he has avoided any tendency to fan the clubface open with his hands and wrists.

Frames #3 show us that the coiling of Tom's hips and shoulders are taking place as a result of his arms and hands swinging the club inward and around. His upper body is following, rather than leading, his arm swing.

Throughout Weiskopf's backswing we see excellent extension of the left arm, which acts as the master lever in the proper swing. We also note that his right knee remains flexed, to act as a brace against swaying and provide him with a good pushing-off position for the start of the downswing. Finally, I'm impressed with the way Tom's forearms roll naturally during the backswing, turning the club into proper position. I see no attempt to quickly lift or otherwise help the clubhead up with the hands and wrists.

In frames #6 we see where the lower part of the body and the legs are beginning to activate the downswing; the knees are beginning to drive laterally towards the target while the hips are about to move laterally, then turn to the left. Note especially how the shoulders are followers to the legs and hips, thus forcing the arms to swing down from well inside the target line and disallowing any premature uncocking of the hands and wrists. By leading the downswing with his legs, Tom conserves the energy built up in his swing until centrifugal force demands that his wrists unhinge and that the right arm begin to straighten just before the clubhead reaches the ball.

One possible criticism of Tom's swing on this particular shot is warranted by the fact that in frames #10 it appears that his right hand has crossed over his left much earlier than happens in the swings of most modern professionals. This indicates to me that Tom's left arm was slowing down too much through impact, thus allowing his right hand to catch up a little too soon.

In frames #11 we find that Tom's head was lowered slightly and moved a bit to the right as a result of the forward action of the lower part of his body and his legs. This is not an unusual result of proper legwork, nor is it damaging to the outcome of the shot unless carried to an extreme.

In the final frames, Tom's weight is now almost completely on his left side and he has extended fully during his follow-through. His completed finish is the natural result of the tremendous accelerated force that he generates through the ball with the 3-iron.

BOBBY NICHOLS

The thing that impresses me most about Bobby Nichols' swing—shown with a 5-iron on the following pages—is his excellent rhythm. He never seems to force the speed of his swing.

In frames #1 of the swing sequences, we see that Bobby plays the ball well forward in his stance, even with the middle irons. This is characteristic of the modern professionals; they rarely play the ball more than two inches from the instep of the left heel, unless they are trying to punch the ball low into the wind or under an obstacle. You will also observe that most good players position the left thumb pretty much straight down the clubshaft so that the back of the left hand faces the target.

During Bobby's backswing we see other indications of the modern golf swing. He swings the club back with his hands, arms and shoulders moving together in a unified action with no attempt to turn the clubface open with the hands and wrists.

Note, too, that Bobby doesn't turn his body quickly or violently, but merely swings his arms freely while resisting slightly with his legs. His knees do work to some degree, but his left heel remains planted, especially on the middle and shorter iron shots. This resistance of the legs and lower body to over-turning stabilizes the body against excessive sideways movement and thus provides full-coiling during the backswing.

In frames #4 it is very apparent that Bobby's left forearm and left hand have really taken over control of the club. The relatively closed position of the clubface indicates that he has pushed the club back with his left arm and hand instead of allowing the right-side counterparts to lift it and cock the wrists.

The excellent extension of Bobby's left arm throughout the backswing is also indicative of the modern player. In the early 1920s, players noticeably bent this arm and thus made a much longer, but less controlled, backswing.

Because Bobby has set the club softly into position at the top with his left side, he avoids any rebounding of the clubshaft that might allow his right hand and arm to take over early in his downswing. He's ready to start down in frames #6 with his legs and left arm and hand pulling the clubshaft back to the ball from well inside the target line, without allowing his right side to throw it to the outside.

Note the flexed position of Bobby's knees throughout his downswing and well into his follow-through. This, too, indicates that he is pulling with his legs and left side. Were he to have commenced his downswing with his upper-right side, his left leg would have stiffened by impact and thus allowed his body to twirl or spin too quickly to the left. Bobby's left knee is farther forward than any other part of his body throughout his downswing, assuring that his left arm and hand lead the clubshaft through the ball. Thus he achieves a late, rather than premature, acceleration of the clubhead through the impact area.

Not until frames #11 do we note much crossover of the right hand, another indication of Bobby's tremendous left-side control throughout his swing, even into his excellent finish position in the final frames.

Lanny Wadkins, an outstanding competitor with great trust in his personal style, seems to be working his way back after a year or two of various injuries and ailments.

In analyzing Wadkins' 7-iron swing on the following pages, the first thing of interest is his head position, which appears to be well to the right of the ball. I'd rather see Lanny address the ball with 'his head more over the ball and his head cocked slightly to the right. Otherwise his address position is fine. The ball is opposite the instep of his left heel. His hands are placed well together on the club, with the back of the left hand facing the target line. His left shoulder is properly higher than his right and his knees are not over-flexed as is the case with many players on shots with a short club.

In frames #2 we can see the takeaway with the clubhead having moved along the target line and then slightly inside without any apparent effort to turn the wrists too early.

In frames #3 the apparent upright position into which Lanny begins to swing the club is unlike that of Trevino. The back of Wadkins' left hand is facing at a right angle to the target, a good checkpoint midway in the backswing. Lanny's right arm is beginning to fold because it is passive, and his left arm remains correctly extended. Frames #4 show the left arm beginning to swing more upward in a very upright swing plane as Wadkins begins to set his hands well underneath the shaft at the top of the swing. In frames #5, we see that Lanny's clubshaft has almost reached the parallel position, giving him a bit more backswing than is actually needed with this club. His wrists have really worked well under the shaft,

however, and his right side is stabilized. His right knee has straightened to some degree but the left is still flexed and ready to move forward and start driving.

In frames #6 we note the apparent weight-shift taking place, with the left knee beginning to move well forward — laterally and then to the left. This leg movement will force the left forearm and hand to move down well from the inside and pull the right arm down close to the body, into a strong striking position for the right side.

We see in frames #7 that the clubshaft is still almost vertical, while the knees have continued to shift towards the target. Lanny's left arm is acting as a master lever to pull the handle of the clubshaft down into a position from where he can finally begin to uncock his wrists (frames #8 and #9). While the uncocking action takes place Lanny's head position remains relatively steady, although he does allow it to turn slightly towards the target and to the left. The left arm and hand maintain a good, stable position through the impact area, with no evidence that his right arm and hand have assumed control of the swing. The right arm extension in frames #11 is the result of the clubhead moving around and up, which also forces the left arm to bend to allow the right side to move freely over and up.

In frames #12 Lanny's weight has shifted almost completely to his left side. His right knee now has pushed forward almost to where it is parallel to the left knee. His head has followed the flight of the ball but the position of his finish is compact, an indication that he has excellent control of his forearms and hands as well as outstanding balance. Finally, like most fine players, Lanny's left heel has hardly left the ground throughout the backward and forward action of his swing.

JULIUS BOROS

Julius Boros is one of the greatest bunker players in the world. One big reason for this is that he applies the same effortless grace to his sand shots that he employs on all other shots. You should always try to make a relatively tension-free swing, but especially so when in sand where the normal tendency is to force the action and over-control the clubshaft. Merely accelerate the clubhead smoothly through the sand and let the force of the sand throw the ball out of the bunker. I see Boros very relaxed at address in frames #1 of the photos on the following pages. He's holding the club lightly, ready to let the weight of the clubhead dictate the tempo of his swing. He's letting his arms hang naturally, with no apparent effort to force an extension of his left arm. He plays the ball well forward in his stance—it would appear opposite his left heel if the camera had been positioned at right angles to his target line. Julius' weight seems about evenly distributed between his feet, but with more settling on the ball of each foot than on the heel. His left foot is withdrawn a bit more than his right from the target line, thus setting his body in a slightly open position so as to allow a more upright swing path.

During the backswing frames we can see that Boros does, indeed, achieve a more upright swing than would be normal on fairway shots. This upright path helps assure that the clubhead will descend on a sharply downward path to the sand and thus slide well under the ball. The proper clubhead path on the type of sand shot he is playing here should be more in the form of the letter "U" than the letter "C" if "C" was laid on its back. This not only assures swinging the clubhead into the sand, but also keeps it moving on the target line longer than if it were swung more around the body.

Boros, like most good sand players, relies heavily on his arms and hands, rather than his legs and body, to swing the club to the top. This helps one maintain better balance in loose sand and minimizes the chance of over-swinging. Note also that Julius retains full extension of his left arm throughout his backswing, another guard against over-swinging.

I'm impressed with the way Boros maintains a very, very steady head position throughout his backswing and downswing. No wonder he has such wonderful control over these shots.

Starting with frames #5 we see Boros beginning to transfer his weight onto his left side. Again, there is no apparent effort to over-control the club with the hands and arms. Boros has great sensitivity in his hands, which allows him to swing, rather than clutch or shove, the handle of the club.

The sliding of the legs to the left on the downswing, though more difficult on sand shots because of the loose footing, is vital. This lower body movement allows you to spank the sand with the flange of the club so that it cuts under the ball, but quickly rebounds upward without digging in too deeply. Without the pulling action that is established by proper legwork, the tendency would be to throw the clubhead into the sand with the arms and hands, probably closing the clubface in the process and producing too deep a cut.

Frames #9 show that Boros has indeed pulled the club into the sand with his left hand and forearm and thus has taken a relatively shallow cut. Were this not true, his clubface would have turned more to the left at this point.

In the finishing frames note that Boros' head does not turn up to look at the shot until the ball is well on its way. Also, he retains a deep knee-flex well into his follow-through, thus avoiding any tendency to lift up and skull the shot. His finish position in the final frames looks almost casual, a further indication of the effortless ease of his over-all sand shot swing.

GEORGE ARCHER

Former Masters champion George Archer will no doubt go down in golf history as one of the game's finest putters. His success on the greens stems from several factors, but particularly from his highly unified hand-arm-shoulder stroking action. His long, rhythmic stroke, with absolutely no lower-body or head movement, remains a model for all who seek improved putting to follow.

One specific mechanical factor that breeds consistency in Archer's stroke is the way he holds the putter in his hands. He holds his left arm and wrist much higher than did the putters of the early 1920s. This is typical of nearly all great putters today. The higher left wrist reduces or eliminates independent rolling of the wrists during the stroke. Although on long putts, such as the 40-footer shown on the following pages, Archer's putter does move inside the target line on both the back and through stroke, I see absolutely no independent opening or closing of the putterface with the hands and wrists.

Holding the left arm and wrist high is achieved by placing the grip of the clubshaft in the channel between the heel and thumb pads of the left hand, rather than beneath the heel pad as is normal for shots with the other clubs. Holding the putter in this fashion automatically sets the puttershaft in a more upright position. This allows the player to position the ball close to the feet so that he can set up to the putt with his eyes directly over the target line, as Archer does.

You will note that Archer sets his hands on the club with the back of his left hand and the palm of his right both facing down the target line. Placing both thumbs down the top of the shaft assures this positioning, which is so important in producing a simple, consistent stroke.

George also holds the putter with a light grip. This is vital in developing maximum feel and sensitivity in the hands.

Archer bends over the ball more than most golfers because of his tremendous height—6'5"—but his overall posture is excellent. His weight is evenly balanced between both heels. He looks directly down on the center of the ball, a good head position for consistent sighting of the line. He bends his arms slightly so that his elbows rest comfortably close to his sides, ready to produce a free—yet compact—stroking action. Finally, he plays all putts with the ball opposite the instep of his left heel, the ideal position from which to impart a true, forward roll to the ball.

The thing I like most about George's stroke is that he never tries to force the movement of the putter with his hands and arms. He lets the putterhead swing freely without attempting to guide or steer it, another big reason for his consistency over the years. His backswing is just long enough to allow him to accelerate the putter through the ball without jerking or forcing or rushing the stroke.

As noted, George's stroke is highly unified with his hands, arms and shoulders working together, thus modifying wristiness which can lead to inconsistency. Throughout the stroke his left hand seems to dominate in controlling the club. The left hand is the leader and the right hand is the follower, never attempting to force the blade as it swings through the ball and toward the hole.